Helping Homeless People: Unique Challenges and Solutions

Edited by

Clemmie Solomon
Peggy Jackson-Jobe

American Association for Counseling and Development
5999 Stevenson Ave., Alexandria, VA 22304

American Association for Counseling and Development
5999 Stevenson Avenue
Alexandria, VA 22304

Cover Design by Sarah Jane Valdez
Cover Photograph by Donna Binder, Impact Visuals
(Fort Bell Street Shelter for Homeless Families, Brooklyn, NY)

Library of Congress Cataloging-in-Publication Data

Helping homeless people: unique challenges and
solutions / edited by Clemmie Solomon, Peggy Jackson-Jobe.
p. m.
Includes bibliographical references and index.
ISBN 1-55620-092-7
1. Homelessness—United States. 2. Social work with the
homeless–United States. I. Solomon, Clemmie. II. Jackson-Jobe, Peggy.
HV4505.H43 1992
362.5'8'0973—dc20 91-47688
CIP

Printed in the United States of America

Contents

Contents

Foreword

Rev. Jesse Jackson

One of the American promises is the right of all of its citizens to life, liberty, and the pursuit of happiness. It is a promise that presumes that its people will be assured that their basic needs of food and shelter will be met. This promise has made America a beacon of hope and a haven for people from around the world. Yet, the greatness of any nation is its ability to deliver on its promise by continuously responding to the real human needs of its citizenry.

I am reminded daily that America is taking hostages in her own land, increasingly with a ransom that is getting too high to pay. Men, women, and children from all walks of life are becoming victims of the growing shortage of adequate and affordable housing.

In recent years, this highly visible population has been crying out for America to fulfill the American promise. Sociologists define this population as a "homeless" people. They may be living on inner city streets, or come from suburban neighborhoods. They may come from back country roads, or from farmlands in America's breadbasket. They are "the least of these" our brothers and sisters: the poor, the less fortunate, the destitute, and the downtrodden.

Many were once working people—teachers, auto mechanics, veterans, and construction workers. Some are highly educated. These are not just nameless and faceless people. They represent families . . . turned out because of lost jobs. Little children . . . with empty stomachs. Some are sick, physically or mentally ill. They may be seen walking our city streets, lying under blankets on sidewalks. They are blocks from the White House.

They may be packed in shelters and welfare hotels. They are those who were lost and forgotten in our unemployment lines, who are now crowding our soup lines. They are part of our present and our future traveling the road of hopelessness and despair. But they are somebody! They are still God's Children! They are hostages! America must turn her energies toward rebuilding a domestic infrastructure that expands the possibilities for improving the quality of life for our homeless.

Today, there are many formal and informal religious and secular groups attempting to address the challenge of homelessness with a variety of helpful initiatives. But we must do more. The homeless do not merely need assistance and shelter, they need homes. With the changing economic times, and the trend toward more austere budgets, homeless people are experiencing greater frustrations and setbacks. It is during times like these that the true test of this country's character is its willingness (it has the ability and the means) to respond to this economic, social, and moral crisis!

Counselors, educators, social workers, psychologists, and related helping professionals have a special responsibility by virtue of their vocational calling to take the lead in addressing this major societal crisis. This book stresses what individuals in the social services can do to help homeless people, how they can listen and try to understand the homeless experience.

This book moves beyond the rhetoric of good intentions and provides practical and useful advice that we can use today to help feed and house the growing number of homeless men, women, and children. They should no longer be ignored. We must shine a bright and hopeful light on the lives of these brothers and sisters.

This problem does not belong to someone else—to another community—but to all of us. We must resist the human temptation to become hardened and insensitive. Our communities, our nation, and indeed our world are only as strong as the weakest, neediest link among us. Here we are offered hope in the face of degradation and despair, and we are taught to become advocates not just for the homeless but for ourselves and our communities.

I recommend this book to counselors, social workers, policy makers, mental health professionals, and to anyone who understands the importance of offering a helping hand to our poorest and most vulnerable—and as a by-product we will help ourselves become better persons and a more noble nation in the process.

We must be careful how we treat the poor, the unemployed, and the homeless. Jesus was born to a homeless couple. Joseph was an unemployed carpenter and Mary was 9 months pregnant with child. Even though they were unrepresented in the government, Rome demanded that they pay taxes and be counted in the census. But when they arrived to pay their taxes and to be registered in the census, the innkeeper (the HUD official of that day) rejected them and told them to go away. Thus Mary and Joseph, a homeless couple, were forced to have baby Jesus in a stable.

We must never look down on the homeless. We never know whom we are rejecting. The homeless man, woman, or child may have a cure for cancer or AIDS in his or her brain. We may be rejecting a teacher, a preacher, a scientist, or a doctor. Today's rejected stone may be the cornerstone of a whole new world order. We just never know.

Finally, while I fully support the social service professions in all of their endeavors to provide help and comfort to the homeless, I must also challenge them to fight for *social change* at the same time. In the final analysis, we do not have a short supply of housing, we have a shortage of political will to build affordable housing for all Americans. And we have inadequate leadership that is unwilling to take this country where it is fully capable of going.

In the end, therefore, homelessness is not a social problem, but a political problem. Thus, I would urge the social service community—at the same time that it provides vitally needed services—to struggle for new political priorities as well. In short we must all be challenged to continue the fight for social justice at home and peace abroad.

Preface

Counseling and related human development professionals recognize homelessness as a very important issue. Developing successful strategies and approaches for addressing the unique needs and concerns of homeless people has become a major goal of the helping professions. Similarly, the seriousness of escalating homelessness has generated greater impetus for counseling and human service providers to obtain scholarly and practical information for helping homeless people. This publication is an attempt by counseling and human development specialists to bridge the gap between problem and solution by providing both contemporary knowledge and selected strategies and approaches designed to facilitate more appropriate helping skills for addressing homelessness. As the title conveys, helping homeless people presents unique challenges, in part because of the growing diversity of homeless populations.

This publication is designed to provide a general but practical guide for educators, counselors, social workers, and related human development professionals to gain a detailed awareness and understanding of homelessness. Corollary to this purpose, information is provided to assist those who work with homeless people in making their efforts more effective and meaningful. Although targeted to helping professionals, this publication should also serve as a valuable resource as well as a nontechnical practical guide useful to the general public.

OVERVIEW OF CONTENTS

This book is divided into 10 chapters. Chapter 1 is an introduction in which Clemmie Solomon discusses the need for helping professionals to commit to addressing the unique needs and challenges of homeless people. He also documents the need for this publication and presents a synopsis of general homeless issues. Further, this publication's special emphases on homeless children and on the importance of building on successes are stressed.

In chapter 2, Joan Alker describes some of the demographic characteristics of the homeless population as well as the social and economic trends that have led to growing numbers of homeless people in contemporary American society. Particular attention is paid to the impact of homelessness on the lives of children, and the characteristics of the runaway and homeless youth population are briefly described.

Although modern American homelessness has emerged on the national political agenda in recent years, the role of the mental health professional has been relatively unstructured and undefined in treating this population. Homeless individuals are not solely the product of deinstitutionalization but can come from all strata of life and have a wide array of emotional problems that contribute to and result from being homeless. Counselors and related mental health providers, in order to be most effective in working with homeless people, need to understand as much as possible about the homeless experience as well as have a firm grounding in clinical treatment strategies.

Accordingly, Ronald J. Koshes in chapter 3 provides a framework for understanding homelessness by addressing mental health concerns in the context of homelessness through an examination of psychological, sociological, and biological aspects. Also examined are assessing needs in order to avoid and combat learned helplessness, the effects of homelessness on family relationships and roles, and the myths about working with homeless people that need to be overcome by mental health professionals.

In chapter 4, Richard K. Yep reviews the role of human service professionals and public policy officials in addressing the homeless situation in America. Legislative history and recent policy proposals at the federal level are explored. Human service professionals are encouraged to utilize their skills as organizers and advocates in helping decision makers to better understand and ameliorate homelessness in America. Practical information is included on organizing coalitions, communicating with those who create laws, and laying the groundwork for effectively working with public policy officials.

Strategies and approaches for counseling and working with homeless people are many and varied. Case management has emerged as an element that is common among these strategies and approaches. Phillis W. Cooke in chapter 5 looks at strategic case management models, their basic functions, and a sample case study as well as at the advantages and disadvantages of these models. Innovative ways of working with the population are cited, and the need for a move from traditional approaches in order to render services effectively to homeless people is emphasized. The chapter concludes with a look at implications for future study.

Alfred L. Cooke, in chapter 6, begins with the basic contention that homelessness is a multifaceted, often intractable, problem that encompasses much more than the absence of a home. This comprehensive presentation on the roles of educators, counselors, case workers, shelter providers, and related helping professionals emphasizes that the solution to the homelessness problem requires a multidisciplined, client-needs-based approach. Also suggested is the impact that disciplines such as teaching, social work, counseling, the ministry, and psychology as well as nonprofessional caring persons can have on solving the homelessness problem. A systematic intervention model is identified.

In chapter 7, Mark Rhyns and Hoang-Oanh Rodgers focus on the unique needs and concerns of homeless women, a particularly vulnerable segment of the homeless population. In addition, these authors discuss the resources required to help these women and emphasize the importance of sensitivity and understanding in any helping interventions. A model program successfully addressing the needs and concerns of subgroups of homeless women is highlighted.

Chapter 8 by Willie Mae Lewis provides practical counseling techniques that can be adapted for curriculum development and training activities. Included are objectives, information for generating discussion, and training exercises.

Peggy Jackson-Jobe in chapter 9 highlights the implications for helping professionals in addressing the unique needs of homeless people and gives a response to the challenge that demonstrates unique solutions and sensitivity.

Finally, chapter 10 provides a comprehensive list of available resources compiled by a research team of the National Association of State Coordinators for the Education of Homeless Children and Youths. Represented on the team were Alabama, Nevada, Pennsylvania, and Vermont.

ACKNOWLEDGEMENTS

In the development of most scholarly projects there are usually several unsung heroes and supporters who give unselfishly of their time and energy. Often they contribute material and technical assistance toward bringing the project to fruition. This publication is no exception and represents the labor of many. The editors would be remiss if their contributions were not acknowledged.

First and foremost we want to give honor and thanks to God, without whose guidance this work would not exist. Sincere appreciation is also extended to family members and friends for their many sacrifices and support. The editors especially want to thank the contributors for their scholarly chapters as well as their hard work and commitment toward meeting tight deadlines. A special note of thanks is extended to the clerical support team of Deborah McClure, Patsy Edinger, and Cynthia Watkins, and to the peer reviewers Wanda Dean Lipscomb, Jane Runte, and Dale Parker-Brown.

The editors graciously appreciate and thank the AACD headquarters staff—Mark Hamilton, Director of Publications, Elaine Pirrone, Acquisitions and Development Editor, Laura Sumner, Publications Marketing Specialist, and Sylvia Nisenoff, AACD Librarian—for their expertise and guidance. A special thank you is also extended to the AACD media committee for its authorization of the publication. Additionally there are a number of people who helped in several ways to make this book possible. They include Russell Davis, Rhonda Gill, Vonda Morris, Mary Solomon, Maria Brooks, Kevin Jefferson, Frank Watkins, Oscar Jobe, Johanna Fisher, George Male, David Huden, and Janice Eldridge.

Contributors

Clemmie Solomon, MEd, is the current president of the Association for Multicultural Counseling and Development (AMCD) and is a National Certified Counselor. He received his BS in history education from Central State University (Ohio) and his MEd in counselor education from the University of Dayton. He is the acting dean of student affairs at Bowie State University in Maryland where he served for several years as the director of counseling and student development and as adjunct faculty member in guidance and counseling at the Graduate School. He has been an active leader with the American Association for Counseling and Development (AACD) as chairperson of the Association's Human Rights Committee and its Government Relations Committee. From 1988 to 1991 he served as a member of the AACD Governing Council. He is a counselor activist on issues of homelessness, aging, and human rights, and he is the recipient of the AACD Legislative Award and the AMCD Professional Development Award. Mr. Solomon was also a member of the Harvard University Class of 1991 Management Development Program.

Peggy Jackson-Jobe, MEd, is the current president of the National Association of State Coordinators for the Education of Homeless Children and Youth. She received her BS in elementary education from Morgan State University and her MEd in administration from Coppin State College. She has worked with parents, students, and teachers for 21 years, serving as an elementary teacher, GED instructor, program facilitator, educational specialist, consultant, and, most recently, coordinator of education for homeless children and youth with the Maryland State Department of Education. As state coordinator, she oversees the education of homeless children and ensures that they have access and success in Maryland's schools. Ms. Jackson-Jobe has received the Governor's Citation for her impressive commitment to working with homeless families in Maryland, the Action for the Homeless Award for outstanding service to Maryland's homeless children, and the Governor's Advisory Board on Homelessness Award for outstanding work on the problem of homelessness as a statewide program administrator.

Joan Alker, MPhil, is the assistant director of the National Coalition for the Homeless, a grassroots-based advocacy organization in Washington, DC. She specializes in issues relating to homeless veterans and homeless families, including educational policy for homeless children, and she has authored a number of reports on homelessness and public policy. Ms. Alker also volunteers with homeless people on the streets of Washington, DC. She received an MPhil in politics at St. Anthony's College, Oxford University, and an AB with honors in political science from Bryn Mawr College.

Alfred L. Cooke, PhD, is associate professor of counseling at Bowie State University in Maryland. He received his BS in secondary education, his MS in guidance and counseling, and his PhD in counseling psychology from Ohio State University. He holds certification as a National Certified Counselor and National Certified Career Counselor. He maintains a private practice in human resource development that focuses on helping individuals and organizations to develop their full potential(s). He has worked in adult graduate degree programs at the doctoral and master's levels with the Union Institute and Vermont College of Norwich University. He has developed and worked with several programs dealing with disadvantaged populations, special needs of women, AIDS risk reduction, drug abuse prevention, international development (resettlement), and career development. Dr. Cooke has a special interest in and has worked with similar problems as they exist in Africa and other developing countries. He is also a National Training Laboratory Institute fellow.

Phillis W. Cooke, MSW, is a Licensed Certified Social Worker, and a Board-Certified Diplomate in private practice in Silver Spring, Maryland. In addition to her clinical practice, she involves herself in consultation to various professional disciplines and programs. A special interest has been assessment of needs and services to homeless people, which led to her development of an Independent Life Skills Training Program for homeless people living in a shelter. Other special interests focus on training and teaching clinical techniques and sensitivity in working with people from varying backgrounds and cultures. Respect for and recognition of the dignity of each person is central to her work.

Ronald J. Koshes, MD, is chief of psychiatry at Kenner Army Community Hospital, Fort Lee, Virginia. He is also clinical assistant professor of psychiatry at the Uniformed Services University of the Health Sciences, F. Edward Hebert School of Medicine, Bethesda, Maryland. He received his medical degree at George Washington University and completed his internship and residency in psychiatry at Walter Reed Army Medial Center. While in residence he was chosen to serve on the American Psychiatric Association's Council on Law and Psychiatry as a Burroughs/Wellcome fellow. He was honored by the Washington Psychiatric Society in 1989 for outstanding service in the field of community psychiatry and received the Al Glass Excellence in Military Psychiatry Research Award at the completion of residency. Dr. Koshes is a board-certified psychiatrist, a member of the Washington Psychiatric Society's Committee for the Homeless, and the author of several journal articles and book reviews.

Willie Mae Lewis, PhD, is currently the executive director of the Institute for Psychological Services in Wilmington, Delaware. She received her BS in psychology and MA in counseling from Texas Southern University. She received her PhD in counseling psychology from Temple University. In addition to service with several community and civic organizations, she also serves on the Delaware State Council on Homelessness and has conducted research on cross-cultural homeless issues. She has been actively teaching as a counselor educator for the past 20 years.

Mark Rhyns, BS, received his BS degree in computer science from Southern University in Baton Rouge, Louisiana. While pursuing a career in software engineering, he developed technical writing skills and subsequently began freelancing as a hobby. His interest in homelessness came out of a genuine concern for the disenfranchised. He is currently employed as a software test engineer at Martin Marietta Aero and Naval Systems in Baltimore, Maryland.

Hoang-Oanh Rodgers, MA, is the coordinator of the Mothers program at the House of Ruth in Washington, DC. She specializes in working with homeless pregnant women, including assisting women in recovery for substance abuse. Ms. Rodgers received a BS degree in counseling psychology at Pennsylvania State University and an MA in counseling psychology at Bowie State University in Maryland.

Richard K. Yep, MPA, is the assistant executive director of the National Association of School Psychologists, and he oversees the areas of government relations, publications, and communications. He was previously employed as the director of government relations for 6 years with the American Association for Counseling and Development where he was responsible for the Association's public policy efforts. Yep has designed and presented public policy workshops in various locations around the country. Prior to coming to Washington and working on Capitol Hill, he served as a Volunteer in Service to America (VISTA) working with native Americans, and he has been involved with education and other human service programs at the local, state, and national levels of government. Yep holds a master's degree in public administration from the University of Southern California and an undergraduate degree from the University of California, Santa Barbara.

chapter 1

Introduction: Addressing the Unique Needs of Homeless People

Clemmie Solomon, MEd

Homelessness is a subject that conjures up many emotions, issues, and concerns. Homelessness is the absence of one of human nature's most basic needs: shelter, a place to live, a place to call home. As the numbers of homeless people increase, concern about and awareness of this complex and far-reaching national phenomenon have grown. Millions of Americans today are either directly or indirectly affected by the growing homeless population.

To address the unique challenges of homelessness, viable strategies and solutions are needed. Issues germane to the subject of homelessness range between the definition of homelessness and the resolution of the homelessness problem. They also include the education of homeless children, race and gender issues, sheltered and nonsheltered homeless people, demographics, causes of homelessness, health care and access to social services, public policy, homeless abuse, approaches to working with homeless people, homeless families, and mental illness and homelessness.

There is currently an abundance of literature pertaining to the topic of homelessness but a dearth of information specifically addressing helping homeless people. Particularly considering the magnitude of homelessness in American society, this lack of information is alarming. The limited research on counseling homeless people and the lack of a knowledge base on the subject among the allied mental health professions means there is a lack of theoretical counseling models from which to develop practical applications for practitioners working with homeless clients.

Helping Homeless People: Unique Challenges and Solutions is designed to provide pertinent information to help those who work with homeless people obtain a greater awareness and understanding of the problem of homelessness and become more effective helpers. It is a general yet practical guide for educators, social workers, counselors, human service providers, and related helping professionals. In addition, it endeavors to serve as a useful tool for the general public.

This book is also the first major publication of the American Association for Counseling and Development on this topic and should serve as a foundation for subsequent research. The allied mental health professions—such as counseling, social work, psychology, and psychiatry—each bear responsibilities associated with facilitating human development. Helping professionals have traditionally been at the vanguard as social change agents and champions of causes to alleviate human suffering. The American Association for Counseling and Development, as the national organization representing the counseling profession, has, for example, developed a clearly defined position statement on the problem of homelessness that identifies several reasons why counselors should be committed to helping homeless citizens (Solomon, 1990). The Association's *Mission Statement* (1988) stipulated a commitment to the removal of barriers to opportunities that may prevent the development and growth of individuals. The Association's *Ethical Standards* (1988) began with the statement that members are dedicated to the enhancement of the worth, dignity, potential, and uniqueness of each individual and thus to service of society. In addition, the AACD Human Rights Committee's position paper (Parker, Wilson, & Ibrahim, 1987) identified a goal concerning undeserved groups; challenged members to develop a sincere desire and willingness to serve all persons to the best of their ability regardless of their racial/ethnic origin, sex, age, disability, creed, sexual/affectional orientation, or social class; and stipulated that AACD is committed to a strong and positive position asserting the rights of all individuals to develop to their fullest potentials. Clearly, from a moral, ethical, and obligatory standpoint, counselors and other helping professionals should shoulder some responsibility to help homeless people. Simply stated, "It's the right thing to do."

Another reason to obtain a greater awareness of homelessness is the impact that the increasing numbers of homeless Americans are having on our social institutions. Schools, churches, shelters, and social service agencies are faced with the need to become more familiar with the characteristics and unique needs and concerns of the diverse homeless population. As with many at-risk populations, it is essential that helping professionals take preventive and proactive measures to effectuate positive results and resolutions to client needs. Playing an advocacy role may be more than justifiable when counselors serve as helpers and social change agents. Gunnings and Simpkins (1972) were pioneers in stressing that counselors should address systemic and structural problems as part of their treatment strategy when working with clients.

Although there have been some attempts at developing theoretical models and approaches for addressing the needs of populations at risk, many conceptualizations have evolved from humanistic modalities. Consider, for example, how Maslow (1970) described humans as having basic needs that are characterized in a hierarchy. Reportedly, lower level needs such as food, shelter, and safety must be met before higher level needs such as love, respect, and self-actualization can be achieved. These higher level needs require better external conditions to make them possible. Therefore, better environmental conditions are necessary to make higher level needs attainable. In the context of a humanistic interpretation of homelessness, it follows that homeless people are more preoccupied with addressing their lower level needs.

Regardless of theoretical preference, some significant realities have hastened the call for human service providers to commit to playing an active role on all fronts in the war on homelessness. Thus, developing nontraditional approaches and recruiting more helpers for the battle against homelessness is essential.

The phrase "There's no place like home," which Dorothy pronounced as she awakened from her nightmare in *The Wizard of Oz*, reminds us of the value of living in our own home. Fairy tales aside, being homeless, without a fixed address, is not an experience just for the millions of people who reside in refugee camps in some far away country or for the twilight children who walk the streets in South Africa. Homelessness is not an experience known only by the millions who sleep on the streets of Calcutta in India or by the nomads who wander the deserts in northern Africa. Homelessness is also a fact of life for increasing numbers of American citizens.

Although it is difficult to determine with accuracy the approximate number of homeless people, there is general agreement that the numbers are steadily escalating. Numerous accounts of the challenge of tracking homeless individuals abound in the literature (Bassuk & Rubin, 1987; Coughlin, 1988; Hagan, 1987; Lockhead, 1988).

At one time homelessness was thought to be a problem only for mentally ill people or the destitute hobos from the nation's skid rows.

Today homelessness encompasses broader populations and includes more women, teenagers, and families with children. A stark reality is that such homeless children are now often found in school systems that in many instances are ill equipped or unprepared to meet their needs.

The Homelessness Information Exchange (1991) has reported on demographics of sheltered homeless people and their causes and trends. The number of homeless people continues to grow, and recent reports indicate that there are as many as 1.6 to 2 million homeless children in the United States. Of the sheltered homeless population, 45% are unaccompanied men; 14% are unaccompanied women; and the remaining 40% are members of families. The percentage of sheltered Black homeless people is slightly more than that of White and non-Hispanics, 44% to 42% respectively. Also reported among sheltered homeless people are high rates of alcoholism, drug abuse, mental illness, and evidence of having experienced domestic violence.

The most frequently identified causes of homelessness are cuts in social services, deinstitutionalization, falling wages, and the shrinking supply of affordable housing. These problems are sure to be around for quite some time. The real question is, What do helping professionals do about them? This publication is an initial step.

HOMELESS CHILDREN

Children represent one of our most valued human resources. Children are therefore a particular emphasis throughout this publication focused on the unique needs and concerns of homeless people. According to one report (Vobejda, 1989), an estimated 220,000 school-age children in the nation are homeless, and a significant number of these do not attend school regularly. Other reports suggest that the number of homeless children is closer to 500,000 or 700,000 (Kozol, 1989; Weiss, 1988). Yet another report (Small, 1987) indicates that there are more than 1 million children in families without homes in this country. Whatever the actual number, the fact remains that it is growing and substantial; and the fastest growing segment, according to *Newsweek* (Karlen, 1986), consists of young children, most of whom are from racial minorities.

Many homeless children are reported to walk the sidewalks with their jobless parents, sit in welfare agencies, play under bridges and along railroad tracks, eat in soup kitchens, and sleep in cars, tents, campers, and public shelters (Dobbin, 1987). Kozol (1988) has also provided considerable data on the health and mortality rates of these homeless children.

Educating homeless children is an important responsibility of many of our nation's schools. It is essential for educators and helping professionals to recognize that homeless children have special educational needs and that numerous related problems may accompany homeless students. For example, one problem can be a child's nonattendance in school because of lack of transportation, family uncertainty about living arrangements, and concerns for the child's safety. Another problem can be a student's nonsuccess in the educational milieu because of lack of stability, lack of references, or lack of a good night's sleep (Maryland State Department of Education, 1989). Other problems include poor nutrition and hygiene, unattended medical needs, neglect and abuse, emotional upsets, developmental delays, no place to do homework, teasing by other students, and feelings of shame. One way to help educators fully grasp the challenge to school systems may be to group the problems facing homeless students into four interrelated areas: (1) transportation, (2) studies, (3) peers, and (4) self-concept (Tower & White, 1989). Addressing the unique needs of homeless children has been and will continue to be a major issue for many of our nation's schools.

SOME ADDITIONAL CONSIDERATIONS

As we begin to explore the unique needs of homeless people, a few additional considerations warrant discussion. Despite the many gloom and doom stories about homelessness in America there are also some successes. One is the case of a former homeless addict from Los Angeles who is now a leading official of California's Department of Alcohol and Drug Programs with an annual salary exceeding $60,000 (Matthews, 1991). Another is New York's medical mobile unit that provides medical care for homeless children. The unit relies on federal and private funds to treat thousands of children living in city welfare hotels and shelters (Kurtz, 1989). In addition: New York and Massachusetts provide transportation for homeless children back to their home school (the school the child attended prior to becoming homeless). Arkansas and Maryland provide after-school tutorial and homework assistance for homeless children at the shelters and nearby libraries. The national program Reading Is Fundamental provides books and reading corners for homeless parents and children residing in shelters in several states. These and other successful, positive stories all too often do not get told or are overshadowed by the negative reports. Helping professionals need to continue to emphasize that the human spirit is strong enough to overcome most barriers to human development and that if the right resources and proper attitudes are brought to bear on the problems of homelessness, many victories and miracles can also be achieved.

REFERENCES

American Association for Counseling and Development. (1988). *Ethical standards.* Alexandria, VA: Author.

American Association for Counseling and Development. (1988). *Mission statement.* Alexandria, VA: Author.

Bassuk, E., & Rubin L. (1987). Homeless children: A neglected population. *American Journal of Orthopsychiatry, 57,* 279–286.

Coughlin, E. K. (1988, October 19). Studying homelessness: The difficulty of tracking a transient population. *Chronicle of Higher Education,* pp. A6–A7.

Dobbin, M. (1987, August 3). The children of the homeless. *U.S. News and World Report,* pp. 20–21.

Gunnings, T. S., & Simpkins, G. (1972). A systemic approach to counseling disadvantaged youth. *Journal of Non-White Concerns in Personnel and Guidance, 1,* 4–8.

Hagan, J. L. (1987). The heterogeneity of homelessness. *Social Casework, 68,* 451–457.

Homelessness Information Exchange. (1991). Demographics, causes and trends. *Homewords, 3,* 1–3.

Karlen, N. (1986, January 6). Homeless Kids: Forgotten faces, *Newsweek,* p. 20.

Kozol, J. (1988). *Rachel and her children.* New York: Crown.

Kozol, J. (1989, March). Darkness in the edge of town. *Parenting,* pp. 57–61.

Kurtz, H. (1989, March 21). For homeless NY children, mobile unit is what doctor ordered. *Washington Post,* p. A3.

Lockhead, C. (1988, September). Compassion and disgust: Dealing with the homeless. *Insight,* pp. 8–18.

Maryland State Department of Education. (1989). *Educating homeless children and youth: How are we measuring up?* Baltimore, MD: Author.

Maslow, A. H. (1970). *Motivation and personality.* New York: Harper & Row.

Matthews, J. (1991, May 28). From derelict to state program official: A California odyssey. *Washington Post,* p. A19.

Parker, M., Wilson, J., & Ibrahim, F. A. (1987). *Human rights position paper.* Alexandria, VA: AACD Human Rights Committee.

Small, M. (1987, December 14). Where Christmas never comes. *People,* pp. 50–60.

Solomon, C. (1990). *Human rights position paper on homelessness.* Alexandria, VA: AACD Human Rights Committee.

Tower, C. C., & White, D. J. (1989). *Homeless students.* Washington, DC. National Education Association.

Vobejda, B. (1989, February). 220,000 schoolchildren lack homes. *Washington Post,* p. 10.

Weiss, S. (1988, February). No place to call home. *NEA Today,* pp. 10–11.

chapter 2

Modern American Homelessness

Joan Alker, MPhil

The 1980s witnessed explosive growth in the homeless population of the United States. This growth paralleled the increasing numbers of persons living in poverty. In 1979, the Census Bureau reported that there were approximately 26 million Americans living in poverty. By 1988, that number had grown to 32 million, an increase of 23%. Shrinking incomes and welfare benefit levels, increasing housing costs, and a loss of affordable housing stock combined to push unprecedented numbers of Americans onto the streets, and into shelters, cars, abandoned buildings, or other makeshift arrangements. Families with children and the working poor swelled the ranks of the homeless population, shattering the old stereotype of the hobo as the typical homeless person.

It is impossible to state with any degree of precision how many Americans experience homelessness on a given night or over the course of a year. Homeless people are difficult to count for a number of reasons. Many are unwilling to be identified as homeless for fear of stigmatization or reprisal—especially in cases where families or individuals are living illegally doubled or tripled up with friends or relatives, or staying in abandoned buildings. Most are simply hard to find: Traditional methods of enumeration do not work for people with no fixed address.

Nightly estimates range from 600,000, a figure from an Urban Institute study (Burt & Cohen, 1989), to 3 million, a figure used by advocates including the Community for Creative Non-Violence and the National Coalition for the Homeless. The Children's Defense Fund estimated that as many as 1.6 to 2 million children may experience homelessness over the course of a year (Mihaly, 1991). The Census Bureau attempted to enumerate "selected components" of the homeless population on a specific night—those living on the streets or in shelters—in 1990 and counted approximately 230,000 persons. The Bureau's findings were roundly criticized at a congressional hearing on the "S-night" count (National Coalition for the Homeless, 1991). Monitoring research reports on the street count paid for by the Census Bureau itself revealed that, on average, the enumerators missed two-thirds of those persons they were trying to count.

Part of the controversy over how many persons are homeless stems from the fact there is often disagreement over who should be considered homeless or, conversely, what should be considered a home. Few would disagree that persons sleeping on the streets or in emergency shelters are homeless. Beyond this group, however, disagreements begin. Should a family that is evicted from their home and sleeping temporarily on a friend's floor be considered homeless or just precariously housed? Should a person institutionalized for severe mental illness but with no address to be discharged to be considered homeless? What about a child placed in foster care who can not be returned to his or her parent(s) because they have nowhere to live?

The federal Stewart B. McKinney Homeless Assistance Act of 1987 (Public Law 100-77) was the first piece of comprehensive federal legislation designed to address some of the emergency needs of homeless people. The Act became law in July 1987, and its provisions have been reauthorized twice since then, most recently during fall 1990. Section 103 (a) of the Act defines a homeless person in this way:

1. an individual who lacks a fixed, regular, and adequate nighttime residence; and
2. an individual who has a primary nighttime residence that is
   a. a supervised publicly or privately operated shelter designed to provide temporary living accommodations (including welfare hotels, congregate shelters, and transitional housing for the mentally ill);
   b. an institution that provides a temporary residence for individuals intended to be institutionalized; or
   c. a public or private place not designed for, or ordinarily used as, a regular sleeping accommodation for human beings.

The definition was intended by its designers to be fairly flexible to account for the varying ways in which homelessness manifests itself in different communities. However, it also leaves open to interpretation the question of who should be eligible for service provided through McKinney programs. These decisions are generally made by the government agencies that administer the funds.

Although the numbers of homeless people are a source of much dispute, substantial growth in the demand for shelter and other services is well documented. The U.S. Conference of Mayors conducts an annual survey of cities and, in 1990, reported a 24% increase in the demand for emergency shelter. The mayors' surveys have reported similar increases in demand for services over the last few years. Seventy percent of the survey cities reported turning away homeless families because of lack of resources; cities also reported a 17% increase in requests for emergency shelter from families (Waxman & Reyes, 1990).

Other studies have examined the increasing numbers of homeless persons in both rural and suburban areas. The National Coalition for the Homeless (1989) investigated levels of homelessness in some smaller communities and found that, for example, in Missoula, Montana, approximately 600 to 1,000 persons were homeless in 1989 with requests for emergency shelter increasing 45% and requests from families increasing 100%. A comprehensive study of rural homelessness undertaken by researchers at Ohio State University found that as many as 6,000 people were homeless in rural areas of Ohio over the course of 1990 (First, Toomey, & Rife, 1990).

The composition of the homeless population has changed dramatically over the last decade to mirror the composition of poor people. A survey of shelters by the U.S. Department of Housing and Urban Development in 1988 found the following characteristics of the sheltered homeless population:

Single men	45%
Single women	14%
Families	40%
Children under 18	26%
Persons with mental illness	34%
Physically disabled persons	11%
Victims of domestic violence	21%

In addition, it is estimated that approximately one-third of adult homeless persons have alcohol or other drug problems (Lubran, 1990), that one-third are veterans (Interagency Council on the Homeless, 1989, p. 248), and that a quarter are working (Waxman & Reyes, 1990). Other important characteristics of the homeless population (which mirror those of Americans living in poverty) are the disproportionate number of minorities and female-headed households as well as the growing number of persons with HIV infection.

RUNAWAY AND HOMELESS YOUTH

A substantial number of older unaccompanied youth should be considered homeless. Many trends have contributed to this growing problem, including parents asking them to leave ("throwaways") and restrictive shelter policies that often do not allow boys over 12 (and sometimes even younger) into family shelters. It is believed that these children now constitute a very significant minority of the overall unaccompanied runaway and homeless youth population, estimated at over 1 million by the National Network of Runaway and Youth Services. A General Accounting Office (1989) report on homeless and runaway youth receiving services through federally funded shelters found that 21% were homeless. The study detailed a number of problems facing this population, with depression being the most commonly reported problem for homeless and runaway youth (61% and 63% respectively). Twenty-six percent of homeless youth in the study had been physically or sexually abused, 36% had experienced parental neglect, and 11% had been exposed to domestic violence. The majority of homeless and runaway youth are White, although Blacks are disproportionately represented in the homeless population.

These children face serious obstacles to obtaining independent living arrangements they can afford, education, and employment. Despite the pervasive personal and social problems found in this population, the availability of services is extremely limited.

WHY ARE SO MANY PEOPLE HOMELESS?

Housing Shortage

The primary reason why people become homeless is because they can not afford to pay the rent. Although substantial numbers of homeless persons may suffer from a range of physical and mental health problems that makes it more difficult for them to maintain stable housing, all homeless people share one characteristic: they are poor. Indeed, homelessness is increasingly becoming a cyclical condition for the poorest Americans who experience very high degrees of residential instability.

A number of trends have combined to create a crisis in the availability of affordable housing for low-income Americans. Foremost is the shortage of low-income units. Between 1970 and 1990, the United States moved from a slight surplus in the number of low-income units (versus the number of existent low-income renter households) to a projected shortage of 4.2 million low-income units (Dolbeare & Alker, 1990). This shortage developed as a result of a number of trends, including massive cuts in the federal housing budget by as much as 80% and a shift from construction of new low-income housing to vouchers and certificates for recipients to use on the open market. Thus, the federal government, until the passage of the National Affordable Housing Act of 1990 (Public Law 101-625), did very little to increase the available stock of habitable low-income units. Gentrification of urban areas and booming investment in expensive residential and commercial real estate are also trends that have contributed to the loss of units.

A particularly important component of the housing stock that has declined significantly during the 1970s and 1980s is single room occupancy (SRO) hotels. These facilities provided private rooms at low rents with shared kitchen and bathroom facilities and were an important source of cheap though often substandard housing for single men, particularly for those discharged from mental hospitals, on fixed incomes, or alcoholic. It is unclear how many SRO units have been lost, perhaps over 1 million, but in Manhattan alone it is estimated that 92,000 were demolished between 1970 and 1982 (Levitan & Schillmoeller, 1991).

In addition to the loss of units, those units that remained were becoming increasingly difficult to afford for poor and moderate income people. Many poor households, especially renters, spend far too high a proportion of their incomes for rents: Although "63% of poor renters paid more than half their income for housing, only 8% of nonpoor renters paid that much" (Hombs, 1990, p. 55).

These problems affect families living in rural areas as well. According to the Children's Defense Fund, 2 million rural households pay more than 50% of their income for housing, and in 1987, nearly 1 million rural households did not have enough money for food after they had paid their housing costs (Mihaly, 1990).

Declining Incomes

As housing costs have gone up, the purchasing power of those dependent on low-wage jobs or public benefits has declined. Between 1973 and 1987, median rent increased by 13% while the income of the poorest 20% of households decreased by 11% (Mihaly, 1990). For those who are working at minimum wage jobs, their earnings are often not sufficient to afford decent housing. A 1989 study by the Low Income Housing Information Service, which assumed that households should spend 30% of their income for rent (the standard used by the federal government), found that two full-time wage earners working for minimum wage could not afford the average rent for a one-bedroom apartment in 44 states (Dolbeare, 1989). The situation for a single parent with children is even more grim. For example, in San Francisco, the least affordable metropolitan area, a single wage-earner would have to earn $17.67 an hour to be able to afford the average rent for a decent two-bedroom apartment. In all of the 25 largest metropolitan areas, a single wage-earner would have to earn twice the minimum wage to be able to afford the average two-bedroom apartment (Dolbeare & Alker, 1990).

Increasingly, jobs that are available to less-skilled workers, including women with children, are found in the service sector, which tends to be low paying with few benefits such as health insurance. Anecdotal evidence suggests that the lack of adequate health insurance often precipitates an episode of homelessness when an accident or illness occurs and results in heavy medical costs and temporary or permanent disability.

Those who rely on public benefits for their income have seen the value of these benefits erode to the point where virtually anyone receiving public assistance is vulnerable to homelessness. Many poor families are recipients of or eligible for Aid to Families With Dependent Children (AFDC), the main federal program providing income support to indigent families with children. AFDC benefit levels and eligibility criteria are largely determined at the state level within federal guidelines. In 1990, in 20 of the 25 largest metropolitan areas, a family could spend its entire AFDC grant on housing and still not be able to cover the costs of a two-bedroom apartment (Dolbeare & Alker, 1990).

Many single homeless persons are eligible for Supplemental Security Income (SSI) benefits, which provide assistance to single persons who are unable to work due to old age and/or mental or physical disability. The level of SSI benefits, which are set by the federal government, are uniformly somewhat higher than AFDC benefits. However, even SSI recipients have extreme difficulty meeting their housing costs: In 12 of the largest metropolitan areas the cost of the average one-bedroom apartment exceeds the total SSI grant.

Contrary to popular belief, the large-scale deinstitutionalization of patients in mental hospitals is not a direct cause of the increasing numbers of homeless persons. The loss of SRO units and the inadequate incomes of persons on SSI are more important precipitants of homelessness. A recent report to Congress by the National Institute of Mental Health (1990) on an investigation of the relationship between deinstitutionalization and homelessness disclosed that deinstitutionalization was not a primary cause of homelessness in general; that most severely mentally ill persons who were deinstitutionalized or never institutionalized are not homeless today; that very few homeless adults (5 to 7% in one study) need acute inpatient psychiatric care; that homeless people with mental illness do not want or choose to be homeless; and that most homeless people with mental illness will accept assistance if it is offered in an appropriate nonthreatening manner.

FACES BEHIND THE NUMBERS: WORKING WITH HOMELESS CHILDREN

It is of critical importance for educators and professionals working with homeless families with children to be cognizant of the social and economic trends that are contributing to increasing poverty and homelessness. Yet it is equally important for teachers and other helping professionals who are just beginning to work with homeless children to be aware of the conditions in which homeless families live and the personal impact of homelessness on families.

Homelessness means more than just not having a permanent place to sleep. For many, homelessness often causes family disintegration and separation for a number of reasons. Many shelters serving families do not allow male parents and boys over 12 (and in some cases even younger) to be sheltered with the mother and the rest of the family. Many parents do not wish to expose their children to the degradation and, in many cases, danger of the shelter system and may leave children with friends and family. Children are sometimes even placed in foster care, or their return home from foster care is delayed, because their parents are homeless or have substantial housing problems.

Children living in shelters, abandoned buildings, cars, and other unsuitable locations generally have nowhere to study, no money to get to school, and no money to buy clothes or adequate school supplies. They face many barriers getting into and succeeding in school, even though federal law mandates the removal of these barriers (see Title VI of Public Law 101-645—the Stewart B. McKinney Homeless Assistance Amendments Act of 1990). Homeless children are also often hungry, undernourished, and more susceptible to communicable diseases. Homeless children are often stigmatized by their peers and sometimes by insensitive teachers.

Homelessness exacts a costly price from children both physically and emotionally. Undoubtedly a critical step for educators and others interested in working with homeless children is to develop sensitivity to the needs and problems faced by homeless children. This can be achieved by working closely with homeless families, by visiting shelters and seeing the conditions in which homeless families live, and by sharing their hopes and fears.

REFERENCES

Burt, M. R., & Cohen, B. E. (1989, July). *America's homeless: Numbers, characteristics, and programs that serve them* (Urban Institute Report 89–3). Washington, DC: Urban Institute Press.

Dolbeare, C. N. (1989). *Out of reach: Why people can't afford housing*. Washington, DC: Low Income Housing Information Service.

Dolbeare, C. N., & Alker, J. C. (1990). *The closing door: Economic causes of homelessness*. Washington, DC: National Coalition for the Homeless.

First, R. J., Toomey, B. G., & Rife, J. C. (1990). *Preliminary findings on rural homelessness in Ohio*. Columbus: Ohio State University, College of Social Work.

General Accounting Office. (1989). *Homelessness: Homeless and runaway youth receiving services at federally funded shelters*. Washington, DC: Author.

Hombs, M. E. (1990). *American homelessness: A reference handbook*. Santa Barbara, CA: ABC-Clio.

Interagency Council on the Homeless. (1991, February). *The 1990 annual report of the Interagency Council on the Homeless*. Washington, DC: Author.

Levitan, S. A., & Schillmoeller, S. (January, 1991). *The paradox of homelessness in America*. Washington, DC: George Washington University Center for Social Policy Studies.

Lubran, B. (1990). Alcohol and drug abuse among the homeless population: A national response. *Alcoholism Treatment Quarterly*, *7*(1).

Mihaly, L. K. (1991). *Homeless families: Failed policies and young victims*. Washington, DC: Children's Defense Fund.

National Coalition for the Homeless. (1989). *American nightmare: A decade of homelessness in the United States*. Washington, DC: Author.

National Coalition for the Homeless. (1991). *Fatally flawed: The Census Bureau's attempt to count selected components of the homeless population*. Washington, DC: Author.

National Coalition for the Homeless. (1991, February). *Homelessness in America: A summary*. Washington, DC: Author.

National Institute of Mental Health. (1990). *Deinstitutionalization policy and homelessness: A report to Congress*. Washington, DC: Author.

U.S. Department of Housing and Urban Development. (1988). *National survey of shelters for the homeless*. Washington, DC: Author.

Waxman, L. D., & Reyes, L. M. (1990). *A status report on hunger and homelessness in America's cities: 1990*. Washington, DC: U.S. Conference of Mayors.

chapter 3

Understanding the Framework of Homelessness

Ronald J. Koshes, MD

Although homelessness has emerged on the national political agenda in recent years, the role of the mental health provider has been relatively unstructured and undefined in treating this population. Homeless individuals are not solely the product of deinstitutionalization but can come from all strata of life and have a wide array of emotional problems that contribute to and result from being homeless. Mental health providers, in order to be most effective in working with the homeless, need to understand as much as possible about the homeless experience as well as have a firm grounding in clinical treatment strategies. This chapter addresses mental health concerns in the context of homelessness by examining psychological, sociological, and biological aspects. The chapter also discusses the importance of assessing needs in order to avoid and combat learned helplessness, the effects of homelessness on family relationships, the role changes that homeless people experience, and, finally, the myths about working with homeless individuals that need to be overcome by mental health professionals.

Notice: The views of the author of this chapter do not purport to reflect the position of the Department of the Army or the Department of Defense. (para 4-3, AR 360-5)

PSYCHOLOGICAL ASPECTS OF HOMELESSNESS

Describing the homeless situation in terms of a disaster is beneficial in developing our treatment approaches. Displacement or losing one's home is a traumatic event. Research shows us that natural or man-made disasters that cause displacement, especially those which result in communities being uprooted and families separated, are among the most traumatic events in an individual's or community's life. Kai Erikson's study (1976) of the Buffalo Creek disaster described the severe emotional trauma caused when a dam broke, killing dozens and devastating many homes. The aftermath of repair and reorganization further increased stress in the community. Both physical and emotional disorders were prevalent, and the social fabric, the bonds that held the community together, failed to provide a supportive and nurturing environment for victims of the disaster.

Moving is another kind of event that can provide insight into homelessness. Moving gives us the feeling that our lives are temporarily on hold. Prized possessions and all the associated familiar amenities that add both comfort and stability to our lives are packed away and in limbo. That favorite coffee mug, the photograph of a cherished family member, a special chair on a porch, which has become the place where the day begins and ends, become crucial when they are missing. Possessions and orientations help anchor us to our environment and provide us with identity.

Someone who is homeless may have a complete loss of identity in the sometimes quick route to homelessness. Without a phone for contact with relatives and friends, a checking account, or a mailing address to receive letters, the homeless person can feel as if he or she has been washed away by a flood and is adrift, alone, unreachable, disconnected from society (LaGory, Ritchey, & Mullis, 1990; Voell, 1987). However, not all homeless are mentally ill (Snow, Baker, Anderson, & Martin, 1986). Some, prone to mental illness because of genetic or psychological factors, might experience decompensation because of financial hardship, living in a shelter or on the streets, and disconnection from family and friends (Mosher & Burti, 1989). Others, already mentally ill, are especially likely to have exacerbations of their symptoms (Lamb & Talbot, 1986; Levine & Stockdill, 1986).

There is great debate about the epidemiology of mental illness in homeless people. Depending on which geographic region is studied, mental illness in homeless people can account for 10% to 70% of this population (Kanter, 1986). Generally, it is accepted that 30% to 40% suffer from mental illness. Of these, 30% to 40% are chronically mentally ill (that is, they have been deinstitutionalized or are at risk for being institutionalized); 30% to 40% have personality disorders; and 30% to 40% have substance abuse problems (Gelberg, Linn, & Leake, 1988).

Homeless people cannot be grouped solely based on their lack of housing. As in most demographic groups, there are fine distinctions that if overlooked contribute to stereotyping of the group and can lead to ineffective delivery of services (Ropers, 1988). For instance, there appears to be a higher incidence of chronic mental illness in women in inner cities, and men have higher percentages of substance abuse problems (Bachrach & Nadelson, 1989; Johnson & Kreuger, 1989; Ryback & Bassuk, 1986; Susser, Struening, & Conover, 1989). Homeless families may suffer economic hardship, and the children may be prone to severe psychological disorders, including learning disabilities and other conduct problems (Bassuk, Rubin, & Lauriat, 1986; Caton, 1986).

Recent studies indicate that with increased psychosocial support at the community level, homeless individuals are able to maintain adequate employment and get housing. They are also able to engage in worthwhile outpatient treatment experiences that keep them substance free, out of mental hospitals, and, more importantly, out of jail (Stein & Diamond, 1985; Wright, Heiman, Shupe, & Olvera, 1989).

Mental health professionals must prepare themselves for working with homeless people. Mental health professionals may have achieved a level of education and economic stability that may be a source of distress in their work with homeless people. It is important to realize that the problems of homelessness are as diverse as the people who are homeless in order to avoid the "blaming the victim" syndrome, in which the homeless person is seen as inept and unable to effect a worthwhile future for himself or herself (Minkoff, 1987). Each homeless person is an individual whose needs are not being met in some fashion. These needs are as unique to that individual as they are to any person seen in a private practice.

Mental health professionals must also go where the homeless people are. The shelters are the best places to find homeless people, and these are often entry points in a city or rural area for social medical and mental health services (Dockett, Daniel, & Knight, 1989). Shelters are where the counselor has the greatest possibility to interact and to make an impact on changing the homeless person's course in life.

ASSESSING NEEDS TO AVOID AND COMBAT LEARNED HELPLESSNESS

Many helping organizations tend to deliver services without assessing the needs of the individuals they serve. This is a dangerous phenomenon. In fact, if the helping organization attempts to deliver services without any assessment of needs, the end result can be dependency on the organization rather than independence and return to normalcy. As stereotypes can be imposed on people, so too can interventions be imposed upon individuals in need of help. The counselor must always keep in mind that he or she is a consultant to the individual and must determine what the homeless person wants and needs to make the world work. Otherwise, treatment will ultimately fail. The goal of any treatment, especially for homeless people, is for the individuals to carry on in a fashion that is as independent as possible (Stein & Test, 1985). Mental health professionals just cannot walk into a community where there are homeless individuals, or into a shelter, and dictate what needs to be done. They must first get to know the community: Where do the people come from? Who are their neighbors and friends? What type of community—rural or industrial, ethnic or mixed—is this? What are the prized values among the population? What specific cultural or ethnic customs and traditions are practiced? What is the shelter itself like? Who runs the organization? Is it committed to any goals or principles? Are these religious or social?

The best way to combat learned helplessness, the process by which an individual loses the ability to exercise independence, starts when the mental health professional first enters the shelter and meets with the shelter manager and the staff who take care of the homeless individuals there. It is important to get to know the key individuals in the organization, learn what their ideas are, and understand how they anticipate the functioning of a mental health professional within their shelter context. Any attempt to deliver services without these basics can result in failure (Koshes & Clawson, 1989). Homelessness is a community's failure to provide for its most needy individuals; thus lack of teamwork and community effort in treating homeless individuals means that homeless people are treated out of context and without consent, approval, and verification from the community at large, and that they will ultimately experience more harm. Time is the factor here: It may take several months to get to know an organization, its people, and the individuals it serves. In working with homeless people, who may be distrustful of any organizational effort to help them, a consistent approach over time is the best way.

SOCIOLOGICAL ASPECTS OF HOMELESSNESS

As already noted, homeless people are diverse and have been grouped together often only for the political agenda of a city, a state, or the nation. Women are a particularly important subclass of the homeless population. Their gender-specific issues are neither well understood nor adequately treated. The rate of chronic mental illness among women in shelters is much higher than among men, as has been demonstrated by many epidemiologic studies. Further, women are vulnerable to being homeless because they are economically disadvantaged and less likely to achieve job or housing stability. They are also more likely to become victims of violence both while sheltered and on the streets. Women generally have a more distrusting attitude toward helping professionals, and they may be especially distrustful of men who try to help them because of past experiences with spouse abuse, child sexual abuse, or adult rape. There is some evidence to suggest that providing group therapy focusing on gender-specific issues better enables women to end their homeless situation (Bachrach & Nadelson, 1989).

Marginated groups often end up homeless—which furthers the downward spiral of their disenfranchisement and therefore their helplessness. Many of the homeless individuals in shelters are drug abusers, suffer from sexually transmitted diseases including HIV infection, are outcasts from their society or from their families, and have nowhere to turn to for support. Therefore, the shelter can be seen as a socializing experience (Grunberg & Eagle, 1990). Properly run and organized shelters can provide the necessary support for individuals to develop ego strength so that they can successfully look for jobs, enter treatment, and move from the shelters into permanent housing. Groups in women's shelters can be an extremely valuable experience, both gender-specific issues groups and nonspecific groups (McWilliams & Stein, 1987). In one group, which involved weekly meetings of shelter inhabitants on a volunteer basis to talk about what it felt like to be homeless and without a job, the voicing of concerns, fears, and frustrations by group members led to enhanced self-esteem. Psychotherapy and medication groups are possible when focusing on living with mental illness and applying adaptive strategies to find a home and job. Such groups allow members to vent frustration and even rage within the therapeutic and supportive setting of the group. The group leader, a mental health professional, is wise to include shelter staff within these groups, not so much as participants but in order to educate them about mental illness and techniques that facilitate mainstreaming homeless individuals. Shelter workers can be more effective in their role when they know more about the problems their inhabitants suffer (Voell, 1987, 1988).

In addition, the rules and regulations of a shelter experience provide the structure often absent in the chaotic experience of homelessness. Checking in at a certain hour, leaving at a certain time in the morning, and participating in the cooking and cleaning tasks of the shelter can provide shelter inhabitants an external structure that will aid them as they develop an internal structure to look for work and housing. There is a pitfall, however, in this approach. Shelter workers must be very clear about their goal to mainstream homeless individuals. Otherwise dependency can develop as a result of the homeless individual becoming an integral part of the shelter's operation. Indeed, some shelters do operate this way for homeless individuals. Because of a particular proclivity for tasks, some homeless people actually become staff members later on. However, this is not a goal of an emergency shelter. A shelter is set up to be temporary housing in times of crisis, and helpers must keep to the task of moving people on toward more permanent housing and a more permanent connection with social and psychiatric services. The counselor's role here is crucial: He or she must work extensively with shelter staff in order to empower homeless individuals and to decrease their dependency. As already noted, helpers can sometimes enfeeble their clients. The counselor needs to meet regularly with staff members to address issues in the role of the consultant and in ways the shelter is working toward moving homeless individuals into more permanent surroundings.

BIOLOGICAL ASPECTS OF HOMELESSNESS

Homeless individuals often have concurrent medical problems. Mentally ill homeless individuals in particular have a higher incidence of medical illness and mortality. Therefore, mentally ill individuals living in poverty are likely to have higher morbidity and mortality rates (Gelberg & Linn, 1988). Additionally, they are more likely to be involved in drug and alcohol abuse and prostitution and other behaviors that are physically dangerous, such as sleeping in the streets, which can lead to exposure, and traveling around in dangerous areas, which can lead to physical violence. The counselor must be always aware of the importance of good medical evaluation and treatment. The isolation that homeless individuals feel may impair their entry into mainstream services, and when a homeless person comes to the shelter, it is often his or her first entry into both mental health services and medical services.

An effective outreach is important. Goldman and Morrissey (1985) described the new era of community mental health as outreach efforts aimed at treating patients/clients on their own turf. Counselors must make regular journeys to the shelters in order to assess the needs of the homeless individuals. Good mental status testing, as well as recognition of physical problems such as diabetes, malnutrition, and other conditions, will make the counselor's work effective. Seeking medical care may be less threatening than referring a person for mental health services and can often introduce the person to involvement in his or her own well being. It is important to get the individual connected to some supportive mainstream services in order to begin building a trusting relationship. Counselors who are not knowledgeable in medical areas should seek the active consultation of physicians in their community who can deliver in-service or volunteer time to travel with the counselor to evaluate patients.

Additionally, the current state of knowledge about substance abuse is that it is in some way genetically based and environmentally determined. This knowledge can remove the stigmatizing aspects of substance abuse from an already stigmatized population. Active education of shelter workers and community leaders may be part of the job of helping professionals as they work to make it as easy as possible for homeless individuals to engage in treatment.

FAMILY RELATIONSHIPS

When people become homeless, their family structure is often disrupted and fragmented. Children and youth are becoming one of the fastest growing segments of the homeless population (see chapter 1), and prevention and treatment efforts are essential in impacting on this problem. To make matters worse, husbands and wives are often separated for the convenience of the service organization and must live on separate floors or in separate shelters. Families may be split up so that the children live with the mother in one shelter and the husband/father lives in another. Family relationships, no matter how dysfunctional, can provide an important arena for the expression of fears and anxieties. For a homeless person, whether mentally ill or economically deprived, the important thing is to express feelings within the context of a supportive environment. Not all families, however, are supportive, but they do hold structure for the individual; and when someone has been uprooted from his or her home or has no place to go, family structure needs to be maintained.

Violence may occur within the homeless family, which can promote further family fragmentation, and shelter organizations can be involved in dealing with the violent person. It is important to remember here that inherent criminality is not the root cause of such violence. The counselor can be very effective in providing interventions that tend to reduce fears and frustrations and allow the homeless person to talk about the experience of being homeless and being away from the family.

It is entirely conceivable that a full range of mental health services can be delivered to homeless individuals and families. For instance, crisis-oriented family therapy can be provided, family meetings can be scheduled, and specific problems can be worked on. Adequate referrals can be made to financial and legal resources as well as to medical and mental health services when needed. Treatment should be aimed at moving the person to a higher level of functioning, psychologically and economically, and reintegrating him or her into society.

ROLE CHANGES

Individuals undergo a number of role changes when they become homeless, going, for example, from prominence to unimportance, productive to unproductive, mainstream to marginated, and independent to dependent. All such changes involve a concurrent loss of self-esteem as the homeless individual struggles to maintain his or her sense of autonomy and purpose in society. Not all individuals will be working toward the same level of autonomy. It is important for the counselor to assess with homeless individuals just what level of functioning they are coming from and what can be done to move them up a notch toward a more independent, productive, and mainstream level of functioning.

MYTHS ABOUT WORKING WITH HOMELESS PEOPLE

Mental health professionals may not want to become involved in counseling homeless people because of preconceived notions about homelessness and street people, because of many negative television, radio, and newspaper reports. Homelessness is a negative attribution, for complex reasons. Take the word *homeless* itself: In America we do not call people who are living on the streets and in shelters *houseless* or *undomiciled*. We call them *homeless*. Using this word makes it apparent that the homeless person lacks those intangible qualities in his or her life that come from having a home, including stability, friendship, security, self-esteem, and social stature. In working with homeless people, helping professionals may find themselves confronting their own ideas and principles about what it means to be productive in society and what it means to be respected and useful in a work setting. Many myths about working with homeless people come from such perceptions, and an in-depth exploration of the myths by counselors individually or within groups of counselors prior to beginning to work with homeless people may help to assure more effective delivery of services. Helping professionals must remain aware of the myths as they continue their work with homeless individuals, questioning their own resistance if they become burned out or angry, and instead trying to focus on an objective needs assessment and empathic service delivery practice.

Myth 1: Homeless mentally ill and seriously mentally ill individuals are treatment resistant. This pervasive myth has reached into the institutions of training for mental health professionals, including psychiatrists, for many decades (Talbot, Bachrach, & Ross, 1986). Professionals providing free time—for example, 1 to 2 hours a week—to see indigent people often find themselves becoming angry with the clients or patients that never show up, show up late, or constantly promise to come in. A clear idea of what is meant by treatment resistance is necessary: Does it mean that the provider has failed to insure adequate access to care? Does it mean that the patient or client is not interested? Or is it a reflection of the severity of the problem?

A story helps to illustrate the falseness of this myth: A patient I had been seeing in the shelters for several weeks on a weekly basis missed one appointment. At the next meeting I asked why he had not come. I felt somewhat angry about his not being there because I had gone out of my way to come into the shelter to provide an opportunity for him to address his fears and frustrations. I thought that he had not come for the appointment because of treatment resistance, that he was manifesting some sort of interpersonal resistance that would impede his treatment. My patient told me that he had had an appointment for ongoing evaluation of his HIV status scheduled several hours prior to our 6 p.m. time. Because that clinic was overrun with patients, the providers there were only able to see patients on a first-come, first-serve basis. My patient had arrived at that clinic at 7 a.m. He was not seen until 9 p.m.!

Such a situation indicates the effort it may take for a patient to make an appointment as well as the high level of ego functioning necessary to organize and orchestrate an appointment with a provider. For instance, the client needs an alarm clock in order to wake up in time for the appointment, or a watch to be able to know when it is time to travel to see the provider. The person also must know how to use the public transportation system, have the appropriate fare for traveling, and have a secure place for appointment slips. If the person has children, then they must be cared for. Time off must be given by the employer. Further, if the person is psychotic, he or she may not be oriented and may be delusional or catatonic.

Our experiences show that when services are provided on-site—as openly and consistently and flexibly as possible—homeless individuals will actively seek out treatment.

Myth 2: Homeless individuals have poor coping skills and are not likely to benefit from psychotherapy or psychosocial intervention. This myth further stereotypes homeless people. As already noted, homeless people come from all social and economic situations and have life histories that are as fascinating and diverse as most other patients, clients, and people in general. In fact, it takes a more highly developed set of coping skills than most people are willing to admit to be able to live within a shelter, often in cramped confines, or out on the street, fending for oneself for food and protection. In fact, a homeless person who is delusional has developed an entire set of coping skills outside of reality, in a psychotic structure that lends support and reality to his or her otherwise crumbling world (Giovacchini, 1977). When a counselor can go into such a situation and provide the structure and support that lends ego strength to the individual, then the homeless person may ultimately be able to progress to a higher level of functioning.

Myth 3: Mental health providers are not effective and can learn nothing in working with homeless people. This argument is used to keep mental health professionals out of the shelter setting and out of the field of working with chronically mentally ill homeless people. Shelters are, in fact, a rich training environment for young professionals as well as an opportunity for already practicing providers to learn about the limits of their ability to help (Knoedler, 1989). The therapeutic changes are small in chronic illness, as in the rest of the mental health field, but they are recognizable in homeless people nonetheless. Getting someone a new set of dentures, providing someone with legal assistance, and helping someone access social security funds can be major accomplishments although they may seem small. The key to effectiveness is building upon the successful interactions of the homeless individual with society, thus initiating the reintegration of the individual. Accomplishments build upon one another and, in an environment of sustained and supportive intervention, gradually lead the homeless person toward greater independence and toward feeling more empowered.

Myth 4: Homeless individuals do not want mental health services. Many homeless individuals, regardless of their origin, feel overwhelmed and frustrated as a result of their displacement, their homelessness. Although many feel the system of care delivery is senseless, bureaucratic, and unsensitive, some homeless individuals appreciate the opportunities within the system to express their feelings (Malawista & Malawista, 1988). Additionally, many are at crucial stages in their lives with regard to drug abuse and dependence and cannot get motivated enough to seek treatment elsewhere. The shelters provide an excellent setting for outreach to these individuals who are "at the bottom of the barrel," who feel like failures, and who often feel unable to motivate themselves. Many are embarrassed. They may indeed be somewhat resistant in the beginning, but nevertheless most homeless clients value the services of helping professionals and look forward to seeing them regularly.

Myth 5: Working with homeless people makes helping professionals feel good. This is the myth that contributes most to the burn-out and disenchantment of service providers. The fact is that working with homeless people can make helping professionals feel bad. Basic values concerning home, family, industry, morality, and prosperity can be threatened as helping professionals meet people who have different values and limited choices on home, society, friendships, or families. Chronic mental illness may so isolate and marginate homeless people from society that interacting with them in a usual meaningful way is difficult and draining. The counselor must have a support group of peers who work in similar situations so that the providers can talk freely about the experiences of working in this deprived environment. Also necessary is to see just how important the counselor is in providing support to the shelter organization and those who work there. Many organizations for homeless people are religion related and may rely on individual gifts of time and money in order to provide help. A large number of such helpers walk away from the experience feeling awful and incompetent. If good work is to be done, the necessary prerequisites for effective counseling must be included, especially the opportunity for exploration of countertransference issues.

SUMMARY

Working with homeless individuals represents a unique task for helping professionals. It means that they must be involved in a multidisciplinary team effort to treat individuals who are impaired in all spheres of life. Working with homeless individuals is not an impossible task. Rather it is the slow and painstaking application of good mental health practice that results in empowering individuals to care for themselves in a unique and changing environment. Coming to terms with the myths of providing mental health care for homeless people enables the mental health professional to more effectively use his or her skills. Additionally, attention must be placed on the provider's ability to continue his or her work. Consultation to shelter staff members and support groups are of extreme importance. However, further research is needed to determine which treatment strategies work best with certain types of homeless individuals and thus aid in delivering quality and effective services.

REFERENCES

Bachrach, L. L., & Nadelson, C. C. (1989). Chronically mentally ill women: An overview of service delivery issues. In J. H. Gold (Ed.), *Treating chronically mentally ill women, clinical insights*. Washington, DC: American Psychiatric Association Press.

Bassuk, E. L., Rubin, L., & Lauriat, A. S. (1986). Characteristics of sheltered homeless families. *American Journal of Public Health, 76*(9), 1097–1101.

Caton, C. L. M. (1986). The homeless experience in adolescent years. In E. L. Bassuk (Ed.), *The mental health needs of homeless persons* (pp. 63–70). San Francisco: Jossey-Bass.

Dockett, H. H., Daniel, J., & Knight, S. B. (1989). *Patterns in homeless history, service needs, and intervention strategies*. Unpublished manuscript.

Erikson, K. T. (1976). *Everything in its path: Destruction of community in the Buffalo Creek flood*. New York: Simon and Schuster.

Gelberg, L., & Linn, L. S. (1988). Social and physical health of homeless adults previously treated for mental health problems. *Hospital and Community Psychiatry, 39*(5), 510–516.

Gelberg, L., Linn, L. S., & Leake, B. D. (1988). Mental health, alcohol and drug use, and criminal history among homeless adults. *American Journal of Psychiatry, 145*, 191–196.

Giovacchini, P. L. (1977). The impact of delusions and the delusion of impact. *Contemporary Psychoanalysis, 13*(4), 429–441.

Goldman, H. H., & Morrissey, J. P. (1985). The alchemy of mental health policy: Homelessness and the fourth cycle of reform. *American Journal of Public Health, 75*, 727–731.

Grunberg, J., & Eagle, P. F. (1990). Shelterization: How the homeless adapt to shelter living. *Hospital and Community Psychiatry, 41*(5), 521–525.

Johnson, A. K., & Krueger, L. W. (1989, November). Toward a better understanding of homeless women. *Social Work*, pp. 537–540.

Kanter, A. S. (1986). Homeless mentally ill people: No longer out of sight and out of mind. *New York Law School Human Rights Annual*, pp. 331–357.

Knoedler, W. (1989). The continuous treatment team model: Role of the psychiatrist. *Psychiatric Annals, 19*(1), 35–40.

Koshes, R. J., & Clawson, L. D. (1989). Working with the homeless: A resident's perspective. *Jefferson Journal of Psychiatry, 7*(1), 60–66.

LaGory, M., Ritchey, F. J., & Mullis, J. (1990). Depression among the homeless. *Journal of Health and Social Behavior, 31*, 87–101.

Lamb, H. R., & Talbot, J. A. (1986). The homeless mentally ill: The perspective of the American Psychiatric Association. *American Journal of Psychiatry, 256*(4), 498–501.

Levine, I. S., & Stockdill, J. W. (1986). Mentally ill and homeless: A national problem. In B. Jones (Ed.), *Treating the homeless: Urban psychiatry's challenge*. Washington, DC: American Psychiatric Association Press.

Malawista, K. L., & Malawista, P. L. (1988). Modified group-as-a-whole psychotherapy with chronic psychotic patients. *Bulletin of the Menninger Clinic, 52*, 114–125.

McWilliams, N., & Stein, J. (1987). Women's groups led by women: The management of devaluing transferences. *International Journal of Group Psychotherapy, 37*(2), 134–153.

Minkoff, K. (1987). Resistance of mental health professionals to working with the chronically mentally ill. *New Directions for Mental Health Services, 33,* 3–19.

Mosher, L. R., & Burti, L. (1989). *Community mental health: Principles and practice.* New York: Norton.

Ropers, R. H. (1988). *The invisible homeless: A new urban ecology.* New York: Insight Books.

Ryback, R. F., & Bassuk, E. L. (1986). Homeless battered women and their shelter network. *New Directions for Mental Health Services, 26,* 55–61.

Snow, D. A., Baker, S. G., Anderson, L., & Martin, M. (1986). The myth of pervasive mental illness among the homeless. *Social Problems, 33,* 407–423.

Stein, L. I., & Diamond, R. (1985). A program for difficult to treat patients. *New Directions for Mental Health Services, 26,* 20–31.

Stein, L. I., & Test, M. A. (1985). The evolution of the training in community living model. *New Directions for Mental Health Services, 26,* 7–16.

Susser, E., Struening, E. L., & Connover, S. (1989). Psychiatric problems in homeless men: Lifetime psychosis, substance use, and current distress in new arrivals at New York City shelters. *Archives of General Psychiatry, 46,* 845–850.

Talbot, J. A., Bachrach, L., & Ross, L. (1986). Noncompliance and mental health systems. *Psychiatric Annals, 16*(10).

Voell, J. W. (1987). *Dislocation, dismay, and privilege: Reflections on the delivery of services to the chronic mentally ill homeless.* Unpublished manuscript.

Voell, J. W. (1988). *Role definition, organizational process, and treatment resistance: Psychiatric services for the homeless, further reflections.* Unpublished manuscript.

Wright, R. G., Heiman, J. R., Shupe, J., & Olvera, G. (1989). Defining and measuring stabilization of patients during four years of intensive community support. *American Journal of Psychiatry, 146*(10), 1293–1298.

chapter 4

Advocating in the Public Policy Arena

Richard K. Yep, MPA

Homelessness in the most prosperous country in the world is a difficult concept for many people to fathom. Affordable housing as well as counseling and support services for those who are homeless should seem to many Americans a wise investment. However, the American dream of owning a home is for many being replaced with the reality of just keeping children and families fed and sheltered. A recurring question among those who advocate for the homeless is How could this happen?

This chapter looks at how public policy has impacted homeless people, the lack of government response to homelessness, who will help, and organizing and coalition building as essential for advocating effective public policy. A concluding section looks to the future. A list of resources helpful to advocates for homeless people is included.

THE IMPACT OF PUBLIC POLICY ON HOMELESSNESS

During the late 1960s, there was a move to deinstitutionalize patients in mental hospitals in hopes of mainstreaming them back into society. Part of the plan included the establishment of 2,000 community mental health centers to help these individuals integrate into local communities (Foscarinis, 1989, p. 5). The deinstitutionalization took place; but due to budget cuts and policy changes, the community mental health center network was never realized, thereby forcing these individuals onto the streets. Then, during the 1970s and 1980s, a growing number of families and children were displaced from their homes because of economic downturns and the lack of public policy addressing the needs of those on the brink of losing their home. In fact, a U.S. Conference of Mayors report (Waxman & Reyes, 1989, p. 28) acknowledged that 36% of homeless people were comprised of families. Add to this the growing numbers of people who were no longer able to qualify for various benefits such as subsidized housing, health care, disability, and social security due to changing budget priorities at the federal, state, and local levels of government. Clearly, a crisis was developing in the late 1970s in regard to the numbers of homeless individuals, families, and children in America. These factors led to an increased activism by advocates for homeless people in the 1980s.

Realizing that services available to homeless people were far from adequate, community leaders, professional groups, and the homeless people themselves began meeting to discuss how best to move federal, state, and local governments toward providing better resources. Both short- and long-term needs had to be addressed, and advocates felt that a change in public policy toward homeless people was necessary.

Public policies are those decisions made by officials that can impact citizens of a particular jurisdiction and economic or social group. The involvement of human service professionals in public policy decisions is imperative if programs with the most benefit to various individuals are to be realized.

In looking at public policy regarding homeless people, it is important to realize that a natural constituency does not exist in most branches and at all levels of government. In fact, in public policy the old adage about the squeaky wheel getting the grease appears to be working against homeless individuals. Without a permanent address homeless people have been denied services such as social security benefits, education, and health care. Further, homeless people have a difficult time seeking representation by elected officials: When people are homeless, they are not likely to contribute to political campaigns or vote. They are also undercounted in the census, and they do not organize themselves into advocacy groups. Thus those who do advocate for—and implement—policies impacting homeless people are not themselves homeless. This means that those most involved with homeless people must assume responsibility for implementing—or advocating for—policies and services that are fair, compassionate, and effective.

Also important for advocates and public policy makers to know is how decisions in other areas of public policy can affect homeless people. For instance, when gentrification of a downtown area allows middle- and upper-class citizens the opportunity for home ownership in redeveloped inner cities of major metropolitan areas, resulting in an increase in the city's property tax base, the displacement of the poor people who will no longer be able to afford living in these neighborhoods must be taken into account. Or, when a governor and/or legislature decides that more funds should go to education, the long-term effect may be better prepared students who can enter the job market with good skills, but the short-term consequence may be less funds for services to homeless individuals and families.

In addition, decisions made by public policy officials should take into account what homelessness costs the government in support services as opposed to what keeping people in their homes by offering assistance (for example, social service, training, education, health care, or financial subsidies) would cost.

The private sector cannot be overlooked in discussing services provided to homeless people, especially when federal, state, and local governments are financially or politically unable to meet the needs of these people. Business and industry in communities throughout the United States have answered the call for help placed by advocates for homeless people. The private sector's interest in helping homeless people is rooted in effective community service as well as good public relations. Many large companies have foundations through which they make grants and donations benefiting homeless people.

Clearly, the role of the private sector in stemming the causes of and providing solutions to the homelessness problem in America will continue to be discussed by corporations, foundations, and other nonpublic entities. If federal, state, and local governments are unable to fund services for homeless people because of a lack of data, the role of the private sector may be to develop reports supporting public commitment of resources for homeless individuals.

THE LACK OF GOVERNMENT RESPONSE

Although homelessness has always been a component of American society, only within the last decade has the U.S. Congress taken a close look at how best to provide services for those without shelter. Beginning in the mid-1980s, housing and other antipoverty advocates began working on bills addressing the issues surrounding homelessness. Emerging from this movement was the Homeless Person's Survival Act of 1986—a bill introduced in the U.S. Congress that was comprehensive in scope and provided both short- and long-term solutions to the homelessness crisis in America. The bill served as a centerpiece around which advocates and elected officials could rally, and various components of the bill eventually passed.

One of the first major efforts on the part of the Congress and the President to address the homelessness issue was the enactment of the Stewart B. McKinney Homeless Assistance Act (Public Law 100-77) on July 22, 1987, subsequently reauthorized on November 7, 1988 (Public Law 100-628). The McKinney Act provided grants to state and local governments for assistance, including shelter, counseling, social services, education, job training, and medical assistance. Unfortunately, the McKinney Act, named after the late Representative Stewart B. McKinney who was a vociferous advocate on behalf of homeless people, has never received its fully authorized level of funding and thus has not met the expectations of those who work on behalf of homeless people.

Other pieces of legislation passed at the federal level included Public Law 99-570, which made benefits available to people regardless of whether or not they had a permanent address, and Public Law 99-500, which made grants available to state and local governments for the creation and operation of homeless shelters.

Propelling these pieces of legislation onto Congress' agenda was in part the growing belief of advocates around the country that the government had an important role to play in providing direction, technical assistance, and funding for those without shelter. However, funding of programs for homeless people has not always been easy to come by because of competing political, social, and economic interests such as the defense buildup of the early 1980s, toxic waste clean-up, the savings and loan crisis, the ever-growing federal debt, and the difficulty of state and local governments in meeting the needs of their constituencies.

WHO WILL HELP?

Who then can be counted on to work on behalf of homeless people in the public policy arena? Because of their role in helping clients and students, many believe that human service providers are in an ideal position to effect positive change for those without shelter. Human service providers who work with homeless people, such as counselors and human development specialists, are more than just technicians trained to work with individuals, couples, and families. An implicit trust has been placed in members of the helping professions. This trust extends beyond the boundary of direct services to those in need. Thus it is imperative that members of helping professions step outside the familiar realm of direct services in order to work with officials who formulate policies and determine funding for services that impact upon homeless people.

The challenge for the advocate working on behalf of homeless people is bringing together the information, the people, and the various sectors of society in order to craft programs benefiting those without shelter. Advocates at the local level, such as the late Mitch Snyder, have been able to focus the nation's attention on the plight of those without shelter via actions such as protests and hunger strikes. Snyder, the driving force behind the creation of the Washington, DC, Center for Creative Non- Violence, was able to attract the media and public policy decision makers by organizing homeless people as well as those who advocated on behalf of homeless people so that they could urge public policy decision makers into action supporting homeless people.

With the continual squeeze on federal, state, and local jurisdictions to provide services for a growing number of interests, it will be increasingly difficult for homeless people to continue receiving even the limited amount of funding now directed toward them. If ever there was a need for those in human services to recommit themselves to advocating on behalf of homeless people, it is surely now. The 1990s will be a critical decade. Counseling and human development professionals can be instrumental in providing public policy decision makers at the local, state, and federal levels with the information they need to enact the services that will help homeless people.

The short-term goal in public policy for homeless people is to make sure that those without shelter have access to the services that will allow them to live in a safe place and to receive counseling, health care, job training, and education. The long-term goal is to look at the roots of homelessness and what can be done to alleviate this growing problem in America, particularly because in the 1990s an increasing portion of homeless people will be comprised of children.

ADVOCACY: ORGANIZING AND COALITION BUILDING

What can counselors and human development specialists do to continue advocating in the public policy arena on behalf of homeless people? Organizing and coalition building are essential strategies. Human development professionals can be a conduit between homeless individuals and those in the public policy arena. Counselors and human development specialists are most likely to deal with those government agencies responsible for providing services such as housing, food, and health care to homeless people, and they can take a broader perspective of the government's actual delivery of services and identify how such services were originally envisioned and planned. With this type of information, advocates for homeless people can better understand how various pieces of public law were crafted and make improvements via amendments in the legislative arena, regulatory changes in the executive (or agency) branch, and litigation through the court system.

Counselors and human development specialists need to realize the important role they can play in advocating on behalf of homeless people. Using skills in consensus building, human service providers can bring together organizations with common concerns regarding homeless people. Traditionally, this type of coalition includes human service, health care, legal, and housing advocates. However, given the changing demographics of homeless people, some nontraditional groups may form into a coalition in order to advocate improved services for some specific group of homeless people. For example, with the increasing number of homeless school-aged children, it behooves school administrators, parent-teacher associations, and teacher unions to work together to ensure education services for homeless children. Another example might be home builders, contractors, bankers, and landlords who could join with other members of the business community and with human service advocates to work on legislation for implementing emergency housing grants and providing special housing loans for those people who are in jeopardy of losing their homes due to layoffs at work or some other catastrophe. Because the homeless population includes growing numbers of elderly people, yet another nontraditional coalition might include a local or state chapter of retired citizens and aging military veterans who are interested in helping those from their generation. By working with human service providers who understand what types of programs are needed for the homeless elderly, such a coalition might be especially powerful, given the high percentage of voters over age 65 in the United States.

Before any type of coalition building begins, however, identification of what the problem is and how to solve it must take place. As groups come together to discuss problems faced by homeless people (or a subset of homeless people), it is important to begin thinking creatively about which groups might be interested in joining such a coalition. Careful planning and preparation are essential in working to improve public policy that impacts homeless people. The ramifications of some type of public policy action go beyond simply providing services. Dealing with public officials and their staffs requires counselors and human development specialists to have a clear understanding of the legislative, regulatory, or judicial public policy process.

Table 1 lists steps that human service providers may find useful in planning a public policy initiative designed to improve services for homeless people. In organizing a particular initiative, human service professionals can review the list and select those items most valuable for their activity.

TABLE 1

Steps in Organizing a Public Policy Initiative

1. Identify the problem.
2. Define ideal solutions.
3. Bring together interested and affected parties who are likely to support the effort:
   - other professionals
   - community leaders
   - homeless people.
4. Brainstorm over which other groups might want to be involved.
5. Discuss the opposition to the initiative and how its concerns might be mitigated.
6. Research the costs to implement the initiative.
7. Develop background materials supporting your issues.
8. Have a clear understanding of the process necessary to enact your initiative.
9. Assign coalition members to various tasks.
10. Identify a spokesperson.
11. Begin seeking communitywide support.
12. Contact public policy makers who will support your idea and seek their commitment to help convince their colleagues of your idea.
13. Develop articles and editorials on your issues for use by the media.
14. Identify businesses and foundations that might be able to help.
15. Keep coalition members informed of your progress on a regular basis.
16. Seek public hearings on your issue.
17. Invite public policy makers to your site (if applicable) for a first-hand inspection of your facility and make sure the media knows of the visit (especially if it would be beneficial to the public policy official).
18. Keep those public policy officials who support you informed of your progress.
19. Be willing to compromise, if necessary, but do not let the opposition know before it is appropriate.
20. Remember to thank supporters (both within the coalition and public policy officials) for their efforts.
21. Do not lose hope if your first effort fails. Simply raising the public's consciousness should be seen as a victory on the road to implementing your initiative and is a good start.

CONCLUSIONS

Implementing public policy beneficial to homeless people between 1990 and 2000 is sure to face serious roadblocks due to cutbacks in domestic programs resulting from the federal budget deficit and from critical budget shortfalls in various states. Public policy officials, whether elected, appointed, or career civil servants, must be shown the data that will convince them of the priority need for bills, regulations, and judicial decisions alleviating homelessness in America.

In addition to providing services to homeless people for immediate needs (i.e., shelter and health care), initiatives must focus on the future—on making housing more affordable, on providing benefits that allow those on the brink of losing their home relief from such a catastrophe, and on helping those with mental and physical impairments to integrate into, and become productive members of, society. Public policy officials must come to depend on human service professionals, such as counselors and human development specialists, for information and help in formulating the good policy that translates into effective services.

One of the best ways to guarantee effective public policies benefiting homeless people is to ensure that those in decision-making positions are sensitive to the needs of that population. Questioning candidates for public office on what they know about the plight of homeless people is one way to find out where each stands on the issue. Those already in office need to be fully apprised of what is happening to the homeless people who fall within their jurisdiction, and they also need to know what the future holds for homeless individuals based on decisions made by federal, state, and local governments.

Without adequate public policy between 1990 and 2000, the homeless population will continue to grow in both large and small cities. As the number of homeless people in smaller communities increases, a greater burden per tax dollar will be placed on these jurisdictions as opposed to major metropolitan areas, which generally have greater resources on which to draw.

There are no easy answers to alleviating the homeless crisis in America. Only a concerted effort that involves those in public policy as well as those who work closely with the issue of homelessness will lead to solutions. Homelessness can no longer be regarded as an issue that only impacts particular groups of people. Data show that those who are homeless become a broader cross-section of Americans each month. If those who are entrusted with helping the less fortunate, such as counselors and human development specialists, are willing to take on the challenge of working in the public policy arena for the betterment of those without shelter, much can be achieved before the year 2000. The challenge is in making sure that the expertise of those on the frontlines is shared with those who craft the policy. Human service professionals cannot expect those in the public policy arena to seek them out; rather, it is apparent from what has been experienced over the past 20 years that information and experiences will have to be made available to (and followed up with) officials if they are to become actively involved in working to alleviate homelessness.

To reiterate: One of the keys to impacting the public policy arena will be the level of knowledge possessed by human service providers on how the system works. Further, it is human service providers who will have to work toward the empowerment of those without shelter so that homeless people can also advocate for their own needs.

REFERENCES

Foscarinis, M. (1989, Spring). Federal legislative and litigative strategies: An overview. *Maryland Journal of Contemporary Issues.*

Waxman, L. D., & Reyes, L. M. (1989). *A status report on hunger and homelessness in America's cities: 1989.* Washington, DC: U.S. Conference of Mayors.

RESOURCES

The following federal agencies, national organizations, and congressional committees are active in providing either services or formulating policies in regard to homeless people. This is not an exhaustive list but rather one offering human service providers an overview of possible resources.

Federal Programs

Community Mental Health Service Block Grants
Public Health Adviser
U.S. Department of Health and Human Services
Alcohol, Drug Abuse, and Mental Health Administration
Rockwall II, 10th Floor, 5600 Fishers Lane
Rockville, MD 20857
(301-443-3820)

Community Mental Health Service Research Demonstration Projects
Office of Programs for the Homeless Mentally Ill
U.S. Department of Health and Human Services
National Institute of Mental Health
Parklawn Building 7C06, 5600 Fishers Lane

Rockville, MD 20857
(301-443-3706)

Emergency Food and Shelter National Board Program
Federal Emergency Management Agency
500 C Street, S.W., Room 710
Washington, DC 20472
(202-646-3652)

Emergency Shelter Grants Program
Office of Special Needs Assistance Programs
U.S. Department of Housing and Urban Development
451 Seventh Street, S.W.
Washington, DC 20410
(202-755-2140)

Health Services for the Homeless
Division of Special Populations Program Development
U.S. Department of Health and Human Services
Health Resources and Services Administration
Parklawn Building 7A22, 5600 Fishers Lane
Rockville, MD 20857
(301-443-8134)

Homeless Children and Youth Education Grants
U.S. Department of Education
Office of Compensatory Education
400 Maryland Avenue, S.W., Room 2004
Washington, DC 20202-6132
(202-732-4728)

The Interagency Council on the Homeless
451 Seventh Street, S.W., Room 7274
Washington, DC 20410
(202-755-1480)

Job Training for the Homeless Demonstration Program
Office of Strategic Planning and Development
U.S. Department of Labor, Employment and Training Administration
200 Constitution Avenue, N.W.
Washington, DC 20210
(202-535-0682)

National Organizations

American Association for Counseling and Development
Office of Government Relations

901 East Capitol Street, S.E., Second Floor
Washington, DC 20003
(202-543-0030)

Center on Budget and Policy Priorities
777 North Capitol Street, N.E., Suite 705
Washington, DC 20002
(202-408-1080)

Children's Defense Fund
122 C Street, N.W.
Washington, DC 20001
(202-628-8787)

National Coalition for the Homeless
1621 Connecticut Avenue, N.W., Fourth Floor
Washington, DC 20009
(202-265-2371)

National Law Center on Homelessness and Poverty
918 F Street, N.W., Suite 412
Washington, DC 20004
(202-638-2535)

U.S. Conference of Mayors
1620 I Street, N.W.
Washington, DC 20006
(202-293-7330)

United States Congress Committees

Select Committee on Children, Youth, and Families
U.S. House of Representatives
H2-385 House Annex II
Washington, DC 20515-6401
(202-226-7660)

Subcommittee on Employment and Housing
Committee on Government Operations
U.S. House of Representatives
B349-A Rayburn House Office Building
Washington, DC 20515
(202-225-6751)

Subcommittee on Human Resources
Committee on Education and Labor
U.S. House of Representatives

320 Cannon House Office Building
Washington, DC 20515
(202-225-1850)

Subcommittee on Children, Family, Drugs, and Alcoholism
Committee on Labor and Human Resources
U.S. Senate
SH-639 Hart Senate Office Building
Washington, DC 20510
(202-224-5630)

Subcommittee on Housing and Urban Affairs
Committee on Banking, Housing, and Urban Affairs
U.S. Senate
SD-535 Dirksen Senate Office Building
Washington, DC 20510
(202-224-6348)

chapter 5

Case Management Models and Approaches for Counseling and Working With Homeless People

Phillis W. Cooke, MSW

Providing services that attend to the needs of homeless people is a recent development in our social system. Unique strategies and approaches have had to be sought in order to render effective services for counseling and working with the homeless population.

This chapter looks at case management, strategic models, the advantages and disadvantages of these models and approaches, practical considerations for counseling and working with homeless people, and implications.

The traditional method of providing services to clients is to contact the client by letter or telephone, or to go to his or her home, and thereby set up an appointment. The client then comes to the service provider at the designated time for services. This method does not work in providing services to homeless people. There is no address to which correspondence can be sent, no telephone to call, no home to visit. Thus, no contact is made, no appointment is set, and no service is delivered.

CASE MANAGEMENT

These simple observations serve to raise our awareness to the need for a different approach to counseling homeless people and providing essential services to them. The case management system has emerged as an essential tool in servicing the needs of our homeless population (Rog, Andranovich, & Rosenblum, 1987).

Case management has nearly as many variations as the agencies that provide it. In some states case management is mandated, in others case management is suggested, and in yet others, case management services are not required at all. Definitions range from the very specific and mandated to the very vague.

Many variables affect the development of definitions, including the state, county, or local jurisdiction involved; the needs identified to be serviced; the characteristics of the targeted population; the system or agency under which services will be provided; the time frame under which the services will be rendered; the availability of funds; and, in some instances, how long the program has been in operation. There is no one formula that is "correct."

It is useful, however, to look at basic approaches to different models and note what is and is not effective in service delivery to homeless people.

The goal of the case management system is to get needed services to the targeted population, in this instance homeless people. To service the needs of homeless people in entirety means, paradoxically, that the system must provide for the unique needs of each client being serviced in the homeless population, and not to "the homeless" as an entity. This can present a substantial challenge.

Although definitions of case management are extremely varied, several functions of case management have been identified and defined (Levine & Fleming, 1987). All case management services include at least one of these functions depending on the setting and the identified purpose of the agency or service deliverer as well as other already mentioned variables. The basic functions of the case management system include:

- Client identification and outreach
- Individual assessment
- Service planning

- Linkage with requisite services
- Monitoring of service delivery
- Client advocacy.

Client identification and outreach is just as implied. Clients to be serviced are identified. In situations where clients who need services may be unable or unwilling to request them, means of seeking out and offering services to a potential client are developed.

Client assessment is a detailed evaluation of the strengths of the person as well as areas of need. The client's mental health, level of functioning, physical health, life style, support network, and need for any variety of services must be accurately assessed if quality service is to be provided.

Service planning results from the assessment that is done with each client. It is crucial that the case manager be involved in the planning stage, whether the case manager is operating with a team or from a one-on-one perspective. In the service planning, the case manager can become familiar with the client's needs and identify any gaps in available services. The case manager may also need to act as an advocate for the client at this stage, should services be unavailable.

Linkage with requisite services means not only referring a client to a service but also providing whatever support or supplemental services are needed to actually get the client to the referred service. This includes such things as accompanying the client to an agency, providing bus fare, or assisting the client in filling out forms. This is obviously a time-consuming process; however, it is necessary if service is to be accessed. Follow-up to assure that clients actually receive needed services is part of this case management function.

Monitoring of service delivery is necessary after linkage has been achieved. This function serves as feedback and a reassessment of the service planning and linkage. Ongoing contact with the service provider and with the client is made in order to assure that the expected service is being received and that the services continue to be appropriate for the client. Clients should be encouraged to evaluate the services they are receiving. As progress is made toward reaching the goals of the service, modification in the service plan may be appropriate.

Client advocacy is needed in order to service the needs of the homeless population. Client advocacy works from two levels: The case manager must work to assist the client in receiving all benefits to which he or she is entitled. The case manager must also work to compel the delivery system to make service accessible to homeless clients.

Client advocacy is very important for homeless mentally ill people, who require a wide variety of specialized services and who have often not been a service priority in our communities. Long-term mentally ill people make up a significant segment of our homeless population, however. For example, one report found an average of 29% of homeless people in selected cities nationwide fell into this category (U.S. Conference of Mayors, 1987). Other studies—with diverse measurement approaches and differences in sampling—have noted a higher range in the percentage of current mentally ill homeless people as well as in those who are "seriously and persistently" mentally ill. According to Tessler and Dennis (1989):

> the range narrows (28–37%) when one focuses on studies which used standardized assessment instruments to determine current psychiatric status (Baltimore, 37%; Los Angeles, 28–33%; Ohio, 31%; and Boston, 29%). The St. Louis researchers also used a standardized assessment instrument and found that 46% of their sample scored above the cutoff point on the Global Severity Index of the Brief Symptom Inventory. However, when they made the distinction between chronic and acute mental illness, they found only 20% of their sample to be serious and persistently mentally ill. (p. 28)

CASE MANAGEMENT STRATEGIC MODELS

Case management programs have been widely used in efforts to provide services to homeless people. The system of case management is so diverse, its strategic models and approaches so varied, that it is impractical to consider any one of them "correct" while considering others "incorrect." Different models and approaches work in different circumstances. They are not "pure" but can provide a point of reference, and they can be grouped into three categories:

1. the therapist/case manager model
2. the team model
3. the broker model.

These basic functions of the case management system, described in the preceding section, vary in these models and can be tailored to the variables existing in any particular program. The case management functions can usually be performed in all three models by counselors, social workers, psychologists, or those in other related fields.

The *therapist/case manager model* assigns each client to one person who is responsible for carrying out all of the case management functions that are to be delivered to the client. This may include such basic survival needs as attaining food, clothing, and shelter. In addition, it may include providing clinical therapy, obtaining financial entitlements on behalf of the client, accompanying the client to a health appointment, designing a treatment plan, assisting with independent living skills, providing job and career counseling, advocating on behalf of the client, and linking the client with other agencies or services in the community.

In this model the therapist/case manager is accountable to a case manager supervisor. A diagram of this model is shown in Figure 1.

Several variations of this model exist:

- Counselors or mental health assistants develop the closest relationships with the clients and perform a significant part of the day-to-day case management functions. Each counselor or mental health assistant is then supervised by the case manager. Although the functions are performed by others, the case manager may function in specifically defined roles such as service planning, entitlement procurement, housing opportunities, advocacy, and monitoring of service delivery.
- Graduate social work, counseling, psychology or nursing students may intern, performing many of the already described case management functions. These interns usually provide services for one school year.
- An intern supervisor supervises and oversees service delivery. This supervisor then reports to the case manager.
- A clinical coordinator supervises the entire team, depending on the institutional system (Levine & Fleming, 1987).

According to one report (Ridgway, 1986), the therapist/case manager model is more appropriate in a stable setting, such as a community center, or when working with a relatively stable group of homeless persons. The team model, then, is more appropriate in outreach work, or with young adults.

The *team model* approaches case management as a function versus an individual. Everyone on the team is familiar with all the client cases, although a team member may work more closely with certain clients or services. Provisions for sharing of information are incorporated into the normal work schedule. Joint conferences may be held weekly to share information formally. Information is informally exchanged as the opportunity or need arises.

The members of a team vary depending on the agency purpose and setting. In a mobile service the team may consist of an outreach team that actively seeks out potential clients on the street and a medical/psychiatric team that provides services to those referred by the outreach team.

The Midtown Outreach Program in New York City is an example. In this program, an outreach team—known as a street team—consists of

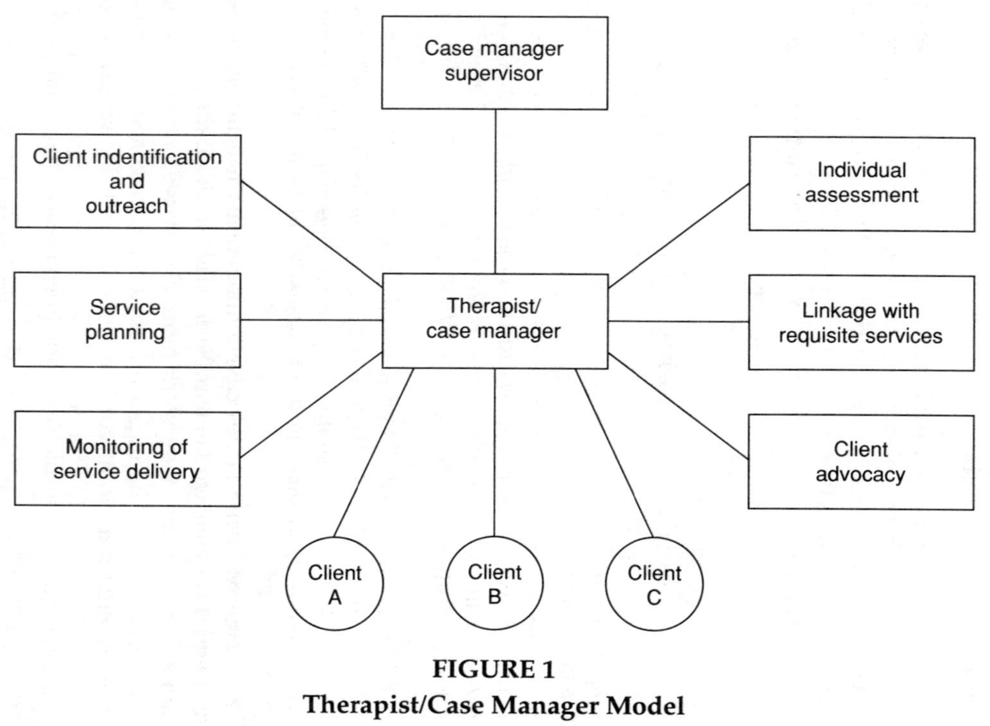

FIGURE 1
Therapist/Case Manager Model

two social workers and a driver. Clinical supervision is provided by a field supervisor. The main goal of each street team is to identify and engage individuals in service. Case management functions are only one of the services offered. The case management functions are shared by all to some degree, though some are more speciality specific than others. In addition to the street team is the medical/psychiatric team consisting of a registered nurse or licensed practical nurse, a psychiatric nurse, a physician's assistant, and a psychiatric aide. The two teams work closely together to refer and provide for medical care and to exchange information on all cases serviced through the program.

Figure 2 is an example of a team model.

In the *broker model* contracts outside the agency are funded for case management services. Funding from state allocations, which may require matching local funds, goes to a state health and/or mental health agency, such as the Department of Mental Health and Mental Retardation, Department of Mental Health, or the State Department of Health and Human Services. The agencies must be able to show that they are performing case management services.

These funds are then used to contract out case management services to local or state governments, who in turn may subcontract with private service deliverers. For example, the case manager may be a counselor in a county facility who is responsible for developing and overseeing the treatment plan while the social worker in the service delivery agency performs all or some of the case management functions.

Figure 3 is an example of how the broker model works.

Practical Considerations

No matter which model or approach is used, there are many practical considerations to note. Many of them are mentioned repeatedly in the literature.

- People who work with homeless people must have a healthy baseline respect for the dignity of every person.
- Any person who has direct contact in working with homeless people must have training in mental health and in handling potentially explosive situations.
- In outreach and in service delivery, provision *must* be made to allow enough time for the development of trust between the potential client and the potential service provider.
- Comprehensive services are needed for homeless individuals and families.

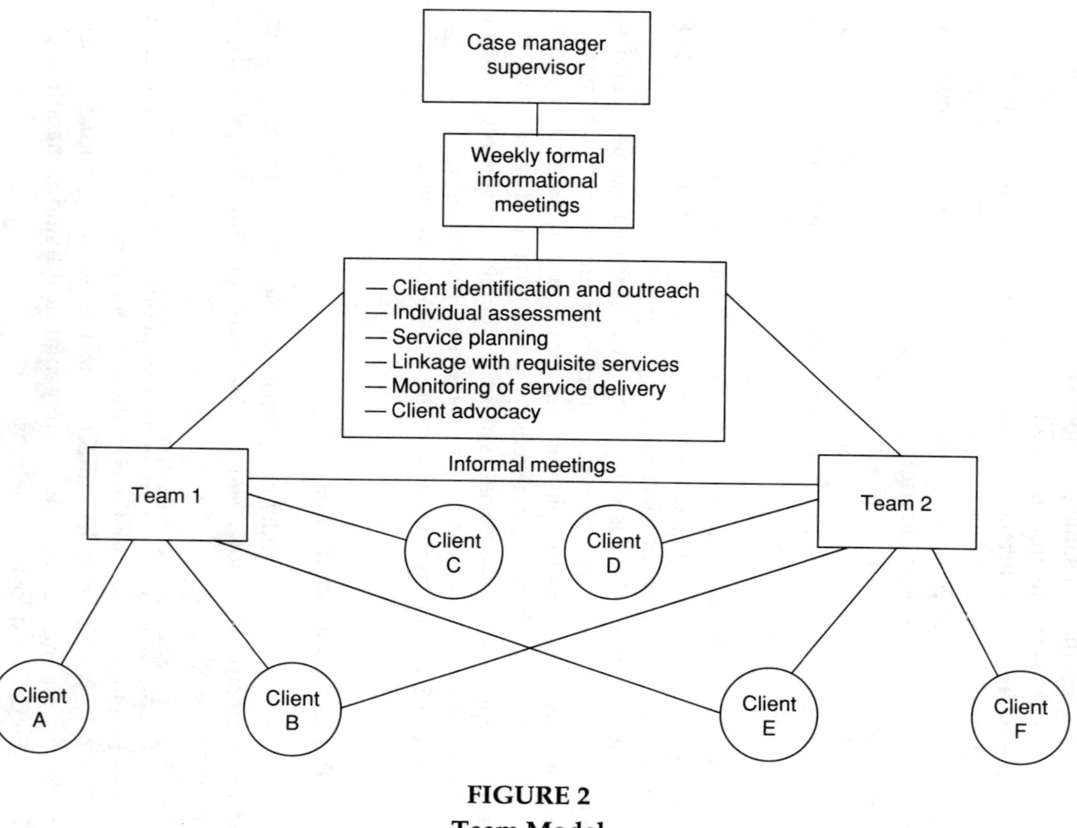

FIGURE 2
Team Model

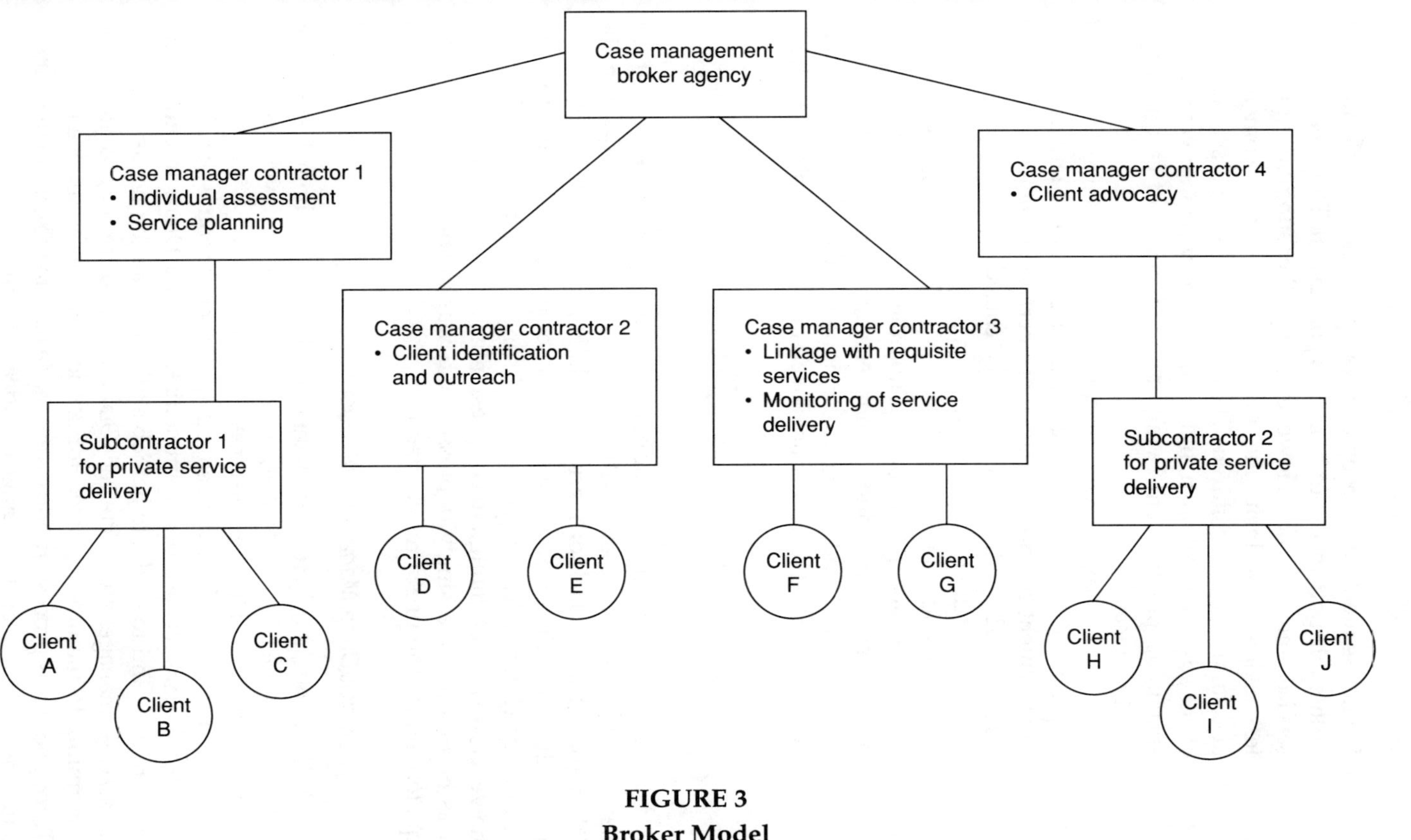

FIGURE 3
Broker Model

- Homeless mentally ill people make up the most visible and most vulnerable portion of our homeless population. They need special services and advocacy. However, many other subgroups of homeless people exist, including adolescents, children, women, men, and families with children. They also need special services and client advocacy. Women and men who may be more capable of sustaining independent living are still in need of case management services.
- Basic needs (food, shower, clothing, temporary shelter) must first be provided before more abstract services (financial management, procurement of entitlements, more permanent housing, medical care, mental health services) can be considered.
- Case management and related services offer low pay, as well as high caseload numbers, and require high and sustained energy in order to get the job done. Thus the importance of servicing our homeless population is not recognized, no incentive is provided for qualified people to continue in this field, and no package is presented to attract new, well-qualified people to the field.

Case Study

Diane cares for her two children after a marriage break-up that left her with loss of income and with a need to make more money in the job market. Diane's lack of marketable skills eventually took its toll on her ability to maintain food, shelter, and clothing for herself and her school-age children. The father provided some support for the children; however, it was not enough to cover essential and ongoing needs. Diane was becoming increasingly depressed and was unable to function adequately under the pressures she faced.

Therapist/Case Management Model

Diane sought help for herself and her children at a homeless shelter. She was assigned to a therapist/case manager who developed a case management plan. The therapist/case manager helped Diane enroll her children in school and introduced her to the school counselor. The therapist/case manager also began immediately to aid Diane in entitlement procurement and to evaluate her job skills and training needs. The therapist/case manager then referred Diane to a job training center while continuing to monitor her need for services as well as service delivery. Throughout this process, reports were made back to the case management supervisor, with useful exchanges of ideas and input.

Team Model

The team driver spotted Diane and her children wandering the streets, and the team approached them. Diane was reluctant to spend time with them. Over a period of several days, different street team members sought out and made contact with Diane and her children. When an adequate degree of rapport was established, the team was able to invite Diane into the mobile unit where an assessment of her needs was made and service planning begun. Providing basic medical care was accomplished in the mobile unit itself by the medical/psychiatric team. Then basic provisions for food, clothing, and shelter were made. Afterwards, outside referrals were made in line with the assessment and service planning.

Broker Model

Diane was referred via the shelter to the Department of Human Services. She was also referred to a tutorial program for her children and to a community career development center for herself. She met with another agency contractor to assess her ongoing income needs and to another subcontractor who helped her detail a plan for meeting these needs. Diane was further referred to the county community mental health center to help with her depression and to help stabilize her emotionally. The broker case manager stayed in touch with all of these contractors and monitored service delivery.

ADVANTAGES AND DISADVANTAGES OF THE STRATEGIC MODELS

Each strategy and approach has its own advantages and disadvantages.

In the *therapist/case management model,* a major advantage for the client is that there is only one person to relate to and who is responsible for accessing all the needed services. This model can cut down on fragmentation of services because the case manager is aware of any gaps in services and can link the client to appropriate services to bridge those gaps.

Another advantage from the view of professional growth and knowledge is that this approach offers the case manager the opportunity to become acutely knowledgeable about a wide range of services and procedures which he or she must access as a function of case management. This model also offers the opportunity for the case manager to do professional networking as he or she comes in contact with people who are responsible for various provisions for services.

A disadvantage of this model of case management relates to continuity of service and arises from the fact that service is based on a trusting relationship established between a professional and a client. Trust must not be overlooked in making provisions to provide effective service delivery (Cooke, 1988). Trust is an important issue among homeless clients not only because of their numerous experiences with various service systems that have not gone well for them but also because of various life experiences in which caution has been essential for their personal safety and survival. Therefore, delivering services to the client in the therapist/case manager model may sometimes not be easy. Disruption in services and gaps in information about the status of services for a particular client may occur if the case manager is ill, on vacation, on leave, or otherwise unavailable for a length of time. This means that whenever there is an absence of or change in case manager, time must be allowed for development of rapport and trust between the client and the new or substitute manager.

A related and readily understood disadvantage of the therapist/case management model is that performance of case management functions is very time and energy consuming and case manager burn-out is a clear possibility.

In the *team model* the major advantage is that the function of case management and service delivery is shared by all. There is flexibility in service delivery. A team member may choose to develop skills in numerous areas but specialize in a particular area.

A client can go to the team member who can best service a particular need. This arrangement still allows for the benefit of sharing knowledge and skills, evaluation, problem solving, and planning with several people from different disciplines. Further, with a team of staff members providing services and sharing the responsibility of working with needy, often long-term clients, the probability of burn-out and staff turnover is reduced.

Because the team model provides for continuity of services in the absence of any particular team member, the client has the opportunity to learn to develop trusting relationships with more than one person. This may aid the client in relating to others with whom he or she must come in contact. However, whether or not this opportunity for the client is an advantage or disadvantage is not clear (Ridgway, 1986). Development of a trusting relationship with a team of people versus with one person is likely to take a longer time. Therefore, the actual service delivery is also likely to take a longer period of time.

The *broker model* has the advantage of providing for coordination of comprehensive service delivery among service providers on behalf of the client. Gaps in availability and/or quality of services may become apparent. Client advocacy may then be needed.

A disadvantage of this model is that it allows perhaps more readily for fragmentation of services. Of course, how successfully and effectively the needs of clients are being serviced depends on the vigilance of the case manager, the number of people being monitored via the caseload, and the definition of case management responsibilities. It also depends on adequate funding. The broker model particularly pulls our attention to the need for planned and structured funding, a lack of which continues to plague delivery of adequate and appropriate services to homeless clients in all models.

IMPLICATIONS

It is a well-established fact that traditional methods of service delivery do not meet the needs of the homeless population. Innovations already developed to meet service delivery needs include mobile units, drop-in centers, and temporary shelters. The different models and approaches to case management presented in this chapter also represent innovative ways to provide service to homeless people.

The task remains enormous. Areas that demand further attention include the following:

- Development of adequate ways to secure funding in order to provide appropriate services. This includes funding through federal, state, and local governments. It also includes provisions for use of Medicaid monies for appropriate services and involves developing policies at all levels of government and in administrations of agencies to make funds available for needed services.
- Development of a clear definition of case management. This involves continued study of the systems that are already operational. It also involves continuing study and research to determine whether a goal should be to have more than one definition of case management by raising such questions as What role do the needs of a local population play in this definition? What about the setting of the agency? What about its purpose? How does the time allocated for service to an individual affect what is reasonable and appropriate case management? Should there be national expectation of case management? Under what circumstances?

Some things are clear about working with our homeless population. This clarity has been brought about through experience and through research. The field is in need of further study. The field also needs follow-up research on studies already done in order to get an accurate picture of what is effective under what conditions and of what innovations must be undertaken.

REFERENCES

Cooke, P. W. (1988). *Report in independent life skills training*. Unpublished report on program for homeless people living in a shelter.

Levine, S., & Fleming, M. S. (1987). *Human resource development: Issues in case management*. College Park: University of Maryland, Center of Rehabilitation and Manpower Services.

National Center on Homelessness and Mental Illness. (1988, May). *Case management with homeless mentally ill persons*. Delmar, NY: Policy Research Association.

Ridgway, P. (1986, July). *Case-management services for persons who are homeless and mentally ill: Report from an NIMH workshop*. Center for Psychiatric Rehabilitation, Sargent College of Allied Health Professionals, Boston University.

Rog, D. J., Andranovich, G., & Rosenblum, S. (1987, May). *Intensive case management for persons who are homeless and mentally ill* (Vol. I). Rockville, MD: National Institute of Mental Health, Division of Education and Service Systems Liaison.

Tessler, R. C., & Dennis, D. L. (1989, February 9). *A synthesis of NIMH-funded research concerning persons who are homeless and mentally ill*. Rockville, MD: National Institute of Mental Health, Division of Education and Service Systems Liaison.

U.S. Conference of Mayors. (1987, May). *Local responses to the needs of homeless mentally ill persons*. Rockville, MD: National Institute of Mental Health, Division of Education and Service Systems Liaison, Program for the Homeless Mentally Ill.

chapter 6

The Role of Helping Professionals: Developing a Strategy for Intervention in Homelessness

Alfred L. Cooke, PhD

Various disciplines have the potential for impacting upon and intervening with the problem of homelessness in America. Educators, counselors, social workers, therapists, ministers, lay persons, and other professionals all have a role to play in alleviating this difficult social problem and in impacting upon and improving the lives of persons who find themselves in crisis because they lack adequate living accommodations and/or are disassociated from their fellow humans. This chapter is designed to help individuals who may come into contact with homeless persons (1) to become sensitive to and understanding of the problem and (2) to identify and develop strategies for intervention. The target of the chapter is any helping professional who feels the necessity of intervening in the life of a homeless person.

Homelessness is an economic, social, and psychological adjustment disorder. Its manifestations are multifaceted and often elusive. Its solutions are similarly diverse. Coming to grips with the economic, social, and psychological components of homelessness as they react individually and upon each other in an individual's life is an important part of identifying a formula for intervention in the homeless condition.

A number of solutions for homelessness are apparent, all of them easily identified, if not as simplistically implemented. Solutions involve creating low-cost housing, creating jobs that pay a living wage, renewing the vitality of the American family, increasing the education level of the population, providing services that anticipate and thus prevent homelessness, and reaffirming the importance of adequate residential treatment facilities for those who need psychological treatment and residential care. Each of these interventions imply an approach that recognizes a multiple causality for homelessness. No two homeless individuals have been impacted by the same environmental or "internal press" (anxiety) and are experiencing the condition in the same way. Intervention must be cognizant of these differences.

This chapter, thus, takes the position that the helping professional working with homeless people must put aside therapeutic rules and approach the homeless person through a counseling intervention that recognizes the need for an eclectic and multidimensional approach—one that attends to, and is directly impacted upon by, a client-sensitive assessment process. This premise has special implications for broadening the base of helping professionals who can impact on the homeless population. These helping professionals include counselors, psychologists, teachers, school administrators, social workers, legal advocates, mental health providers, nurses, doctors, psychiatrists, and any other individuals who might come into contact with a homeless individual either on a limited or a continuing basis. The model described here has implications for all of these individuals.

DIVERSITY OF HOMELESSNESS

An approach to intervention with homeless people must recognize the diversity that exists in the homeless population, both in terms of the population characteristics and the crises that have led to homelessness. Definitions of homelessness encompass descriptors that include lack of shelter, income, social support, or affiliation with others but are not agreed to universally (Rochefort, 1986, pp. 293–294). Levin and Haggard (in Rochefort, 1986, p. 294) noted other definitions as well:

> Bassuk (1983) describes homeless as more than the lack of a home; it is a metaphor for profound disconnection from other people and social institutions. The Alcohol, Drug Abuse, and Mental Health Administration (ADAMHA) (1983) defines homelessness as "both (the) lack of adequate and permanent shelter and (the) absence of community and social ties." According to these broad interpretations, the homeless population includes not only persons on the streets, but also shelter residents and people boarded temporarily in welfare hotels.

Levin and Haggard also noted (in Rochefort, 1986, pp. 294–295) that because of the lack of a precise definition of homelessness, it is practically impossible to estimate the numbers of homeless persons in the nation. The U. S. Department of Housing and Urban Development (HUD), for example in May 1984 estimated that there were 250,000 to 300,000 such persons while the U. S. Department of Health and Human Services (DHHS), using extrapolated figures from local studies, estimated that there were 3 million homeless persons, thus indicating that approximately 1% of the population was homeless during the same period. What we have here is a failure to communicate. Closer scrutiny of the two sets of figures indicates the lack of an agreed-upon definition of homelessness. HUD used figures closely tied to the actual accessibility to a physical structure, whereas DHHS considered homelessness in the broader sense of "disconnectedness and disaffiliation."

Long and Jacobs (1986, p. 4) pointed out that homeless people do not fit the traditional profile: the White male, over 40, with a drinking problem. Instead, they indicated that in New York children from homeless families are the most numerous type of homeless person. Single men are the second most numerous. They also listed other populations that are highly represented in homeless ranks:

- Single adult men
- Single adult women
- Parents and their children
- Victims of domestic violence—mostly women and children
- Mentally ill individuals
- Ex-offenders who have been released from jail or prison
- Veterans, especially those of the Vietnam War
- Alcoholics and drug addicts
- Young people without job skills
- Young people running away from home
- Young people who have "aged out" of foster care
- Elderly people
- Immigrants—documented and undocumented.

About the only descriptor on which most authors on homelessness agree is that there are two clearly distinguishable groups of homeless persons: homeless people who enter that status because of crisis or change in their economic situation and homeless people who are mentally ill (Long, 1988a, b, c, d; Long & Jacobs, 1986; Morrissey & Dennis, 1990; Rochefort, 1986). Both groups suffer the agonizing ravages of isolation and poverty; however, mentally ill homeless people have been identified as a particularly vexing problem for society. The major issues for this group are their dual disenfranchisement, both from society and from service providers. The typical situation is one in which mentally ill persons are excluded from programs designed to serve homeless people, and homeless people are screened out from services designed for long-term, severely mentally ill persons (Rochefort, 1968, p. 293).

Homelessness does have several somewhat universally agreed upon causes (Long & Jacobs, 1986, pp. 1–58). These include:

- Deinstitutionalization without needed community supports
- Inadequate income supports
- Fragmentation of services systems
- Lack of affordable housing
- High unemployment
- Complexity of a social system that hinders the ability of people to utilize support services
- Structural unemployment
- Family breakups and disintegration of the family structure
- Stigma of mental illness that prevents individuals from integrating/reintegrating into society.

There are tremendous implications in these classifications for intervention by helping professionals in the plight of homeless people.

A further classification offers a more manageable set of strategies, however. The causes of homelessness can be grouped under four major discipline headings: economic, social, psychological, and institutional. Table 1 details homeless interventions that have been identified from the literature under each heading (Axleroad & Toff, 1987; Long, 1988b, c, d; Long & Jacobs, 1986; Morrissey & Dennis, 1990; Rochefort, 1986; U. S. Conference of Mayers, 1986).

Only a cursory attempt is made in Table 1 to be mutually exclusive or definitive in the listings under each category. Rather, what Table 1 provides is a succinct listing of possible interventions that the professional may choose from in identifying a means of intervening with the homeless person.

TABLE 1
Intervention Needs of Homeless Persons

Economic	*Social*	*Psychological*	*Institutional*
Housing Income Employment Money management Food Clothing Protection from weather Filling out job application Transitional Housing Shelter Residential alternatives Financial assistance Public housing Public benefits Work assistance	Family support Escort to services Socialization skill development Values Conflict crisis planning Interpersonal relationship skill development Family support Personal hygiene Prevention Enhancement Advocacy	Vocational counseling Self-esteem Mental health Substance abuse counseling Crisis skills Psychiatric and medical evaluation care and rehabilitation Safety Behavioral modification Self-awareness Treatment Prevention Enhancement	Education medical H.S. equivalence Alternative institutional settings Supportive services Help assessing services Outreach Rehabilitation services Legal services Health services

Note: This table represents a compilation of the range of interventions identified as necessary in working with homeless people. The list is taken from the full review of current literature. © Cooke 1991

ROLE OF HELPING PROFESSIONALS

It is not enough to say that the role of helping professionals in intervening with homeless people is to use their skills in the most effective way possible to alleviate the suffering caused by homelessness. That role differs depending upon the profession and professional training of the intervening individual, that is, educators and mental health providers will each attempt to focus on intervening in ways appropriate to their discipline and training.

The professional literature is replete with comprehensive and elaborate institutional (bureaucratic) approaches to the homeless problem (National Resource Center on Homelessness and Mental Illness, 1990a, b, c; Rog, Andranovich, & Rosenblum, 1987; Toff, 1988; U.S. Conference of Mayors, 1986). Many of these approaches attempt to meet the needs of specific populations by responding with focused interventions. For the most part this approach is marginally effective in meeting both institutional needs and the needs of delimited homeless populations.

The human services delivery system seems confused about what it should be doing in intervening with homelessness. The fact that standardization of interventions has not been adopted by the human services delivery system speaks to the multiple causality and multifacetedness of the problem.

> Human services achieves its objectives in large part through its intervention methods, yet there is no methodology of intervention design. Despite this lack, human services practitioners and researchers regularly face problems for which solutions must be adopted. By one means or another, intervention must be developed. (Thomas, 1984, p. 15)

Interventions with homeless individuals are particularly a concern for the human services and for helping professionals because of the fact that every intervention tends to be unique and to break new ground. Just considering the intervention needs for homeless people identified in Table 1 gives a feel for the problem of developing helping strategies. Approaching the problem of intervention with homeless persons requires that the helping professional develop a methodology that can be adjusted systematically to meet the diverse and unique individual needs of clients. Without a framework of intervention, helping professionals will find themselves floundering to identify appropriate approaches each time they are confronted with a new client.

Change Objectives

In order for helping professionals to focus clearly on the intervention process, it is necessary to be clear about what outcomes are being sought in the intervention process. Intervention with homeless persons must provide for the great diversity of homelessness causality through strategies that meet the unique needs of the population. The goal of intervention for homeless people is change of some kind that will either enhance or positively "disrupt" an unenhancing life style. Objectives include remediation, enhancement, competence, education, prevention, advocacy, resource provision, and social control. Change objectives must be tied closely to causality. Causality is such a powerful knowledge base that failure to identify it clearly and tie it directly to the change objective is likely to lead to failure of the intervention process.

Thomas' paradigm of change objectives (1984, pp. 30–31) has implications for intervention with homeless individuals. Missing from the paradigm are two most important elements: decision making and empowerment. Following is Thomas' model (reprinted by permission of Sage Publications, Inc.) enhanced with these two additional components to provide a more comprehensive set of change objectives with special implications for the change needs of homeless people:

- **Remediation**—Intervention directed toward altering a problem that is a source of difficulty for the client. For the homeless person remediation might involve reassessing values, modes of decision making, and outlook on life; correcting self-esteem issues; resolving inappropriate coping mechanisms; and becoming more realistic about dependence on self.
- **Enhancement**—Intervention directed toward improving functioning above an already satisfactory level. Most homeless persons have skills and abilities that may be unused or inappropriately used. Enhancement builds upon what is already in place and moves the homeless person to a succeeding state of survival. Enhancement changes include identifying family resources and pulling them together until they are more effective in helping the individual, or improving information and decision-making skills.
- **Competence**—Intervention directed toward strengthening the client's ability to handle not only an existing difficulty but also a variety of difficulties in a given area, including those that may arise in that area in the future. Competence skills for homeless persons involve dealing effectively with bureaucracies, money management, crisis management, and interpersonal relationships.
- **Education**—The presentation of information to facilitate understanding in an area of intervention. Education or reeducation change skills for homeless persons involve learning new job skills, day-to-day handling of resources, dealing with bureaucratic procedures, self-awareness and self-esteem building, and parenting effectiveness.
- **Prevention**—Intervention directed toward eliminating potential difficulties before they arise or become sufficiently problematic to require remediation. Homeless persons seem, in many cases, not to be able to anticipate crises. Learning crisis management is essential to their coping. Prevention of homelessness requires an attention to identifying low-cost housing, creating jobs, renewing the family, gaining education, and increasing residential treatment for the homeless mentally ill.
- **Advocacy**—Speaking up for and taking other actions on behalf of the client to protect the client's rights and to pursue client interests. Homeless advocacy involves everything from aiding the individual in dealing with the bureaucracy to advocacy on behalf of changing national laws. The issue of increasing availability of quality residential treatment for the mentally ill home-

less is a priority policy in need of advocacy. Similarly, efforts to increase the availability of low-cost housing presents us with a timely policy issue.

- **Resources**—Provision of such resources as food, clothing, shelter, money, or medicine. For most of us our home is the repository of our resources. When we do not have resources, then a home (or address) is key to gaining those resources. For homeless persons the absence of an address means they can not accumulate resources and also makes them ineligible for help from agencies that supply such resources because they do not have a permanent address—a Catch 22 that keeps many homeless persons destitute and homeless.
- **Social control**—Intervention directed toward protecting the clients and/or society, generally through provision of special residential arrangements. Society's rules and programs are designed for middle-class needs. Such needs involve maintaining a document trail. For the most part, absence of documentation puts homeless people at a disadvantage for entering and receiving help from the "system." It puts them outside and often at odds with the society. Change involves balancing the need for social control and order with fulfilling the needs of the individual homeless person. The latter has more often than not suffered at the expense of the former.
- **Decision making**—Provision of directed opportunities to acquire skill in gathering information and using it to make enhancing decisions. Many homeless persons find themselves in their predicament because of an inability to garner information and to make choices based on a systematic analysis of that information. Change in this behavior involves learning how to make appropriate decisions based on balancing need against risk involved in pursuing different needs.
- **Empowerment**—Gaining information and using it for self-enhancement; increasing the level of self-reliance. Empowerment is the ultimate goal of change for the homeless person. Empowerment involves much of what is discussed in the other change objectives. The homeless person is likely to need to look at all of the change objectives at some time in order to take control of his or her life and never return to a homeless state.

All of these change objectives have significance for homeless people. The last two, decision making and empowerment, which are added here by the author, have special emphasis. As with any strategy, the change objective should be chosen carefully and negotiated with the client. This is particularly important because of the characteristics of homelessness. Homeless persons have a distrust of bureaucratic interventions and "do gooder" sympathies. That distrust is based in a failure to include the homeless person in the planning of the therapeutic intervention. Homelessness is so appalling to us as human beings that many well-meaning individuals have but one objective for homeless intervention: to remove the persons from the homeless situation and to make them fit the accepted middle-class norm—with a fixed address, with a family regularly living under the same roof, and with somewhat lasting and ongoing relationships. For homeless persons, that may be too lofty a goal, at least initially. For them the goal of intervention may include more basic issues, such as where to get a bath, locating a safe place to sleep for the night, and getting a meal.

A Client-Needs Perspective and Systematic Planning

The helping professional needs to be sensitive to both the precursors of homelessness and the specific needs of the homeless person. Fennell and Docket (in Morrissey & Dennis, 1990, p. 116) emphasized that because of the multifaceted problems presented by most homeless persons a *client-needs perspective* should be taken by the helping professional. Client need precludes a reliance of helping professionals on "canned," nonindividualized approaches to intervention. *Systematic planning* has been identified as a useful approach for developing interventions in the human services and human development areas (Cross et al., 1975; Herr & Cramer, 1988; Toch & Grant, 1982; Weissman, 1978).

> A systematic approach to program planning rests on the concept of systems analysis, which in turn is concerned with the examination of the interrelationships among the parts of a system in order to formulate goals and objectives. Science, the defense establishment, and industry have used systems analysis and related methodology for several decades to make complex, interactive units manageable and more amenable to monitoring and evaluation. (Herr & Cramer, 1988, p. 186)

Systematic planning seems a tool well suited to the multifaceted problem of homelessness. The remaining sections of this chapter thus attempt to take what we know about the homeless condition and place it in the perspective of a model that has implications for any helping professional confronted by the homeless problem. The model has implications for the teacher who may see only a limited number of homeless children in an entire teaching career and the mental health provider or social worker who may be working on a daily basis with homeless persons.

A client-needs perspective relies heavily on an individually developed intervention strategy based on a survey of the homeless person's needs in the context of the helping professional's skills and comfort level. To indicate that the helping professional must examine each client's needs may seem greatly to complicate the intervention process because it is likely that most helping professionals will not on a continuing basis come into contact with homeless persons. Professionals such as teachers, counselors, school administrators, and clinical case workers are likely to see such persons on a varying, often limited schedule. Such a schedule does not lend itself to developing coping skills that can be used on a continuing basis. It is necessary, therefore, to identify not a process of intervention but a mode of identifying an individually developed intervention strategy that any helping professional can call on in intervening with homeless persons. The client-needs perspective provides such a mode of developing an individual strategy.

MANAGING HOMELESSNESS

The problem of intervention in homelessness is a problem of management. The effective manager is one who can determine appropriate data and develop strategies based on that data. Kepner and Tregoe (1981, p. 20) provided a data-based model for dealing with decision-making situations that has significant implications for the development of intervention strategies with homeless people. They suggested that there are four basic questions to which any management problem must provide answers in order to determine an appropriate solution. These questions are patterns of thinking which all humans use, and evolutionists point out that such thought processes are at the basis of the natural selection process found in the animal kingdom. These processes can be called into play for problem solving. Kepner and Tregoe (1981) identified these basic patterns of thinking as follows:

What's going on?
Why did this happen?
Which course of action should we take?
What lies ahead?

The client-needs perspective assumes that the helping professional needs the answers to these four questions. Based on the results of this survey an intervention strategy can be identified. The four, reworded questions provide the necessary inquiry for developing a strategy of intervention with homeless people:

> What is the situation with respect to the client's homelessness? (What's going on?)
> Why is the client homeless? (Why did this happen?)
> What is the most appropriate strategy that will alleviate or eliminate the homelessness? (What course of action should we take?)
> What can be done to lessen or eliminate the likelihood of recidivism? (What lies ahead?)

1. **What is the situation with respect to the client's homelessness? (What's going on?)** The question seeks to know the background of the person's homelessness, what the homeless person is dealing with at the time of the homelessness crisis, and what has brought the individual to the present state. Seeking this information helps us to better understand what the effective variables are that led to the homelessness and, once identified, to eliminate them or enhance the individual in some way such that he or she is able to cope in enhancing ways in spite of these variables. Seeking this information also enables the helping professional to better gear the intervention strategy to the needs of the homeless person. Are there social, psychological, economic, or institutional variables that have led to the situation?

   Unfortunately, most helping professionals assume that homelessness is cured by locating physical housing. But as already indicated, homelessness is more than housing: it is a disconnectedness, a separation from support systems. Finding a homeless person a physical shelter is a response to the symptom of homelessness and begs the question of causality. Identifying causality and giving it a name immediately identifies a means of eliminating the cause and, ultimately, the homelessness.

   This question also offers an opportunity for helping professionals to evaluate their own skills and confidence in coping with an intervention with the homeless person's issues. Helping professionals should be very introspective and realistic about what they can do. They should not feel a sense of failure if the decision is made not to try to intervene personally. Referral to an appropriate other source is in itself a very viable intervention strategy. Helping professionals should, however, put together their own directories of referral agencies that may be unique to their immediate area.

2. **Why is the person homeless? (Why did this happen?)** Basically there are two reasons why individuals tend to be homeless: crisis or change in economic situation and mental illness. Intervening with the homeless person requires a clear delineation of which of these conditions has led to the homeless situation. The individual who is mentally ill needs intervention mainly from the psychological and institutional-based helping professionals. Quite often this means an *in loco parentis* approach to the client's needs, wherein the individual must give up certain rights in order to get help. Mentally ill homeless individuals need intervention ranging from advocacy in dealing with the bureaucratic system to institutionalization. In either extreme the assumption is that individuals can not care for themselves and need others to provide varying degrees of care—depending on the nature of the mental illness.

   As a policy issue, mentally ill homeless persons present a special problem for the helping professions. Many of them could benefit from institutionalization, either for short- or long-term care. Unfortunately, in the 1960s institutionalization came under negative local and national scrutiny. The result was that many mentally ill persons who needed and could benefit from institutional care were put out onto the streets without adequate preparation, coping skills, or supports. It is perhaps time that a reevaluation of the need for institutionalization on a wider scale be placed on the policy consideration agenda.

   For the helping professional the issue is one of getting a determination of when institutionalization might be appropriate and helping the client to locate a sensitive and caring facility that can provide appropriate intervention and treatment.

   The individual who is homeless because of crisis or change in economic situation finds him- or herself at the mercy of circumstances in the environment. What is usually required in this individual's situation is a change in the environment or the development of skills for coping with the environment. Crisis implies a loss of control by an individual. Regaining that control is often sufficient to eliminate the homelessness. Many individuals who lose control of their environment often lack enhancing coping skills. Such skills can be learned so that when crises occur they do not have such a devastating impact.
3. **What is the most appropriate strategy that will eliminate or alleviate the homelessness? (What course of action should we take?)** Strategies involve positive action. Once the background

of the homelessness is known, and why the homelessness has occurred, a systematic plan for alleviating the problem can be put together. Table 1 presented strategies that have been used with homeless individuals as identified in the professional literature. It should be a fairly easy step to move from survey data (the answers to questions 1 and 2) to identifying one or more of these strategies for intervening with a specific homeless person (client).

A course of action should be relatively straightforward and focused. It should work toward elimination of one or two manageable variables that have contributed to the homelessness. The individual who is young, on the streets, and panhandling for food because he or she has "aged out" of the foster care system and has a whole gamut of needs from economic, social, psychological, and institutional sources. However, the focused need might be location of transitional care, or removal from the "mean streets," as a prelude to the bigger issue of developing adult independence. The former can be worked on immediately; the latter may require more planning and long-term effort. Choosing a course of action carries a heavy burden of prioritizing according to any immediate threat to the safety of the homeless person.

4. **What can be done to eliminate the likelihood of recidivism in the future? (What lies ahead?)** Perhaps the opposite of What's going on? (the first question) is What lies ahead? This fourth question seeks to identify areas of concern and mechanisms that will prevent the homeless person from becoming homeless again in the future. It attempts to anticipate problems and to provide means of eliminating them before they occur. Planning for future outcomes requires foresight and development of new coping strategies in anticipation of future events. Such anticipation carries with it a heavy reeducation burden, both internally and externally/environmentally. Learning how to evaluate information and to make decisions is a major variable in successfully anticipating the future. Homeless persons tend not to be able to anticipate future events and to plan for the unknown. Many find themselves in their homeless conditions because they made wrong decisions. An effective intervention strategy needs to include an attempt to deal with information and to make appropriate decisions. Getting information and learning how to use it—empowerment—is a major theme in helping homeless clients to deal with the future.

MAKING THE PROCESS WORK!

The helping professional working with homeless people has to assume a somewhat eclectic approach to the intervention strategies used. Eclecticism, by its very definition, identifies a process that is client based. It does not, however, obviate the importance of process. The process outlined in the four questions can be formalized into a step-by-step approach, into a systematic planning process that is descriptive and developmental. The process has eight steps that can be placed along a progressive continuum:

- **Identification of *background* and problem-related characteristics of the client**. The helping professional needs to gain as much information as necessary to help the client understand what the issues are that might impact upon the homelessness. Helping professionals have a better chance of empathizing with the client and identifying appropriate strategies when they have knowledge of the precursors of the individual's homelessness. A major piece of information involves identifying whether the homeless person is mentally ill or is homeless because of crisis. The progress of the intervention takes a slightly different direction, as defined earlier, once this information has been garnered.
- **Identification of the *needs* of the client**. Needs should be related to background issues. What are the immediate and long-term deficits that contribute to the homelessness? Basic needs such as medical care, food, and hygiene can be dealt with for the short term. Needs for permanent housing or residential treatment require planning and concerted effort on the part of the helping professional. Clients should be included at every step in identifying their needs. Helping professionals should negotiate needs with the client when there is a discrepancy between those which they see and those which the client has identified.
- ***Rationale* of the intervention**. Why are you doing what you have chosen to do? Helping professionals need to be clear in their minds about the theoretical base from which they are operating when working with the client. Identifying an appropriate change process to be pursued satisfies this step. Is the intervention to involve remediation, enhancement, education, prevention, advocacy, resource provision, social control, decision making, empowerment, or some combination thereof? Goals and objectives for the intervention should be identified based on this rationale.
- ***Goals and objectives* of the intervention stated in measurable terms**. What measurable accomplishments does the intervention

want to produce? Goals and objectives should be tied directly into the fulfillment of needs that have previously been agreed to.

- *Alternative processes*. What are the possible things you will do in intervening? What are the specific processes that will be used in meeting each goal and its objectives? Alternative processes are actual activities that the client and/or the therapist will undertake in meeting the identified needs. Processes might include support groups, medical assessment, educational assessment, and career counseling. The helping professional should rely on resources available in the community for identifying alternative processes.
- ***Evaluation* criteria (plan)**. How will you know you have been successful in the intervention? One way for the helping professional to remain focused is to identify the expected outcomes of the intervention. These become the mode of determining success of the intervention. Evaluation might involve identifying the level of coping with crises before and after the intervention and looking at longevity in remaining out of the homeless situation after the intervention. The important issue is that the helping professional be able to identify formative and summative processes that indicate the impact of the intervention.
- *Milestones*. What steps should you expect as the intervention proceeds? Milestones should be identified for the process and for the client. The intervention should be logical and progressive. A calendar of activities that specifies the progress of the intervention should be developed. This calendar should be as specific as possible with acceptable low and high performance completion dates. The client should be made aware of the milestones that have been established and monitored to assure compliance.
- *Persons responsible*. Who will be responsible for the different components of the intervention? Every action or intervention process should have a specific individual identified as to responsibility. Responsible persons include the client, the helping professional, and any other individuals who may impact on the treatment process.

A helpful activity for the helping professional, especially for those who may not confront homeless persons (clients) on a regular basis, is to delineate these eight steps in columns and fill in the pieces, thus producing a flow chart of activities that can be observed and reviewed. In the early phases of using this process some degree of time may be required. But as use becomes more regular, much of it will become an internal processing, and the necessity of writing it down will be diminished.

SPECIFIC ROLES OF HELPING PROFESSIONALS IN INTERVENING WITH HOMELESS PEOPLE

This chapter began by clarifying just what characteristics were possessed by homeless individuals and continued by identifying strategies and systems for individuals who are trying to intervene with homeless people. Now we apply what has been suggested to specific intervention situations with specific helping profession disciplines.

Educators

Educators may include all professionals who work within the school settings, for example, teachers, administrators, school counselors, and nurses. Educational professionals are likely to confront the homeless problem because of identification of children of homeless people. The trend toward having the school counselor assume responsibility for taking the lead in school-based interventions was an inevitable outcome of the increase in homelessness.

The problem of homelessness is exemplified in the school setting in one of two ways: (1) the family that has been "set out" through eviction and (2) the chronically homeless family that moves into the school district because of a previous homeless move. These two extremes require different strategies. For the temporarily homeless family the role of educators should be to be supportive of the child and the family and to provide information and referral as requested by parents. Temporarily homeless families tend to be in a state of turmoil because of dealing with the immediacy of the problem. Once the immediate problem is resolved, these families will disappear into the normal milieu of the school. Sensitive and concerned teachers and administrators who are able to make exceptions to normal school rules will be greatly beneficial in helping such families through this kind of crisis.

Quite often the situation is that the child who is homeless is not the one who reveals the homeless situation. Such information often comes from other children because of their normal tendency to discuss each other's circumstances. Sensitivity and tact should be used by the school in these circumstances to assure the child's privacy and confidentiality.

The chronically homeless child who comes to the attention of the school often presents chronic school-related problems: numerous absences, poor academic performance, poor socialization, poor personal hygiene, and disciplinary problems. These problems are likely to be the result of the fact that the homelessness has produced many relocations and not allowed the child to develop a sense of belonging in any school setting. Such children often have little supervision at home because parents are unable or unwilling to parent effectively. Chronically homeless children often lack self-esteem and self-discipline.

The school's response to these children should be one of focusing on the academic, attendance, socialization, hygiene, and disciplinary deficits through targeted intervention programs. The key issue for the school should be to attempt to arm homeless children with as many coping mechanisms as possible during the time that they are there, with full realization that they may be in the school for a short period of time. The school that finds itself dealing with significant numbers of homeless children should consider developing specialized intervention programs specifically focused on these children.

School records are a special problem for the chronically homeless child. Since these children move from school to school so often, records should be more detailed and descriptive so that future teachers will be better able to estimate how to help transitional homeless children.

In working with homeless children there is no place for "turfism." Each area in the school must coordinate its efforts with all other areas so that there is a concerted attempt to meet the real needs of homeless children.

In addition to dealing with the school deficit needs of the children, the school should be aware of and have an ongoing relationship with social welfare and social service agencies that have experience with chronically homeless children. It is necessary for the school to pass along to these persons other than academically related problems because they are better equipped to be responsive.

Shelter Providers

Shelter providers have their roles defined by their very titles: they are responsible for providing, usually on a short-term basis, housing for homeless persons. Homeless shelters have a reputation for being dirty, inhumane, and insensitive to homeless persons. Providers have a key role to play in humanizing these shelters. Remembering that homelessness is not an inherent part of persons who are homeless serves providers well in their relationships with homeless persons. Assuring security and respect for residents are two additional roles that providers can play.

Shelter providers are in many cases the only contact that the homeless person has with the bureaucracy. For this reason, being alert to and seeking out ways to "hook" the homeless person on getting other help is an essential role for providers. Providers should be caring and concerned about their residents. Their empathy can be the motivation for getting the homeless person into the system where help is available. A comprehensive directory of referral sources and knowledge of social agency procedures will be beneficial to the providers.

Case Workers

Social case workers have skills in focusing on the environmental variables that may impact on homelessness. Case workers must assume responsibility for assuring a realistic environmental perception in homeless persons and provide them with the resources to traverse their environment successfully.

Therapists and Counselors

Therapists and counselors have the greatest possibility for impacting upon the present and future coping of homeless persons. At the beginning of this chapter homelessness was defined as an economic, psychological, and social adjustment disorder. It is a disorder that lends itself to clinical and therapeutic treatment. Therapists and counselors have the skills required to empower homeless persons to take control of their environment through becoming self-aware and self-enhancing.

Lay Persons

Perhaps the most potent group that can impact on the plight of homeless people consists of those who have no particular professional skills but who are caring human beings. The average person in America today will come into contact with the homeless problem. Calling into play the natural instincts we all have when we see another human being in trouble is the key to this group's intervention. Homeless people are like any of us. In fact, homelessness has been defined as *missing two pay checks*. By that definition, but for luck we could all be homeless. Lay persons should make themselves knowledgeable of the issues in homelessness and learn what resources are available for intervening in the problem. Volunteering to house and feed homeless persons is a very special commitment.

CONCLUSIONS

In another time homelessness might not have been allowed to become the problem that it is today. The disintegration of the social support system that was so significantly a part of earlier societies, especially in America, has led to an obviation of our concern for our families and fellow humans. Because an automatic process of dealing with the problem no longer kicks in as in earlier periods, now there must be a somewhat unnatural approach to the issues of homelessness. Thus the growth of the social service and helping professions has resulted. Yet neither is able to deal with homelessness in as efficient a way as did close-knit families and societies. The result is that formal approaches must often be put in place.

Homelessness is a multiple causality problem with many-faceted issues. The helping professions must be sensitive to the fact that homelessness must be approached on an individual basis. Any individual who comes into contact with the homeless problem has a responsibility as a human being concerned about other human beings to intervene in ways that call upon whatever skills he or she may possess. The nonprofessional individual can help by being knowledgeable about the issue and having available referral resources that can be given to the homeless person.

It is only when all Americans return to a time when we assumed that we all have responsibility for aiding those less fortunate than ourselves that the problem of homelessness will be permanently remedied.

A final word of caution: We have suggested here a process that involves people helping people to resolve homelessness in this country. We have noted, however, that eliminating homelessness will not happen, no matter how much people are willing to help each other, if the economic issues of homelessness are not met. America does not have available low-skill, decent-wage-paying jobs; low-priced housing; decent and clean residential institutions for the mentally ill; or a political climate willing to confront the basic issues of homelessness. Sadly, it does not appear likely that such will be available in the near future. Advocacy must thus be one of the major interventions that those concerned about the homeless should undertake.

REFERENCES

Alcohol, Drug Abuse, and Mental Health Administration (ADAMHA). (1983). *Alcohol, drug abuse, and mental health problems of the homeless—Proceedings of a roundtable*. Rockville, MD: Author.

Axleroad, S. E., & Toff, G. E. (Eds.). (1987). *Outreach services for homeless mentally ill people: Proceedings of the first of four knowledge development meetings on issues affecting homeless mentally ill people*. Silver Spring, MD: Macro Systems.

Bassuk, E. L. (1983, November 6). Addressing the needs of the homeless. *Boston Globe Magazine*, pp. 12, 60ff.

Cross, K P., Valley, R., et al. (1975). *Planning nontraditional programs*. San Francisco: Jossey-Bass.

Herr, E. L., & Cramer, S. H. (1988). *Career guidance and counseling through the life span: Systematic approaches*. Glenview, IL: Scott, Foresman.

Kepner, C. H., & Tregoe, B. B. (1981). *The New Rational Manager*. Princeton, NJ: Princeton Research Press.

Levin, I. S., & Haggard, L. K. (1986). Homelessness as a mental health problem. In D. A. Rochefort (Ed.), *Handbook on Mental Health Policy in the United States* (pp. 293–310). New York: Greenwood Press.

Long, L. A. (1986). *A curriculum for working with the homeless mentally ill*. New York: Author.

Long, L. A. (1988a). *Helping homeless families: A training curriculum*. New York: Author.

Long, L. A. (1988b). *Program descriptions of consumer-run programs for homeless people with mental illness* (Vol. 1). New York: Author.

Long, L. A. (1988c). *Program descriptions of consumer-run programs for homeless people with mental illness* (Vol. 2). New York: Author.

Long, L. A. (1988d). *Consumer-run self-help programs serving homeless people with a mental illness* (Vol. 3). New York: Author.

Long, L. A., & Jacobs, E. L. (1986). *A curriculum for working with the homeless mentally ill*. New York: Author.

Morrissey, J. P., & Dennis, D. L. (1990). *Homelessness and mental illness: Toward the next generation of research studies—proceedings of an NIMH-sponsored conference*. Bethesda, MD: National Institute of Mental Health.

National Resource Center on Homelessness and Mental Illness. (1990a). *The National Resource Center bibliographic database search—families and children*. New York: Policy Research Associates.

National Resource Center on Homelessness and Mental Illness. (1990b). *The National Resource Center bibliographic database search—health and health care*. New York: Policy Research Associates.

National Resource Center on Homelessness and Mental Illness. (1990c). *The National Resource Center bibliographic database search—outreach*. New York: Policy Research Associates.

Rochefort, D. A. (Ed.). (1986). *Handbook on mental health policy in the United States*. New York: Greenwood Press.

Rog, D. J., Andranovich, G. D., & Rosenblum, S. (1987). *Intensive case management for persons who are homeless and mentally ill: A review of community support program and human resource development program efforts* (Vol. 2, State and local project summaries). Washington, DC: Cosmos.

Thomas, E. J. (1984). *Designing interventions for the helping professions*. Beverly Hills, CA: Sage.

Toch, H., & Grant, J. D. (1982). *Reforming human services: Change through participation*. Beverly Hills, CA: Sage.

Toff, G. E. (1988). *Self-help programs servicing people who are homeless and mentally ill*. Silver Spring, MD: Macro Systems.

U.S. Conference of Mayors. (1986). *Beyond food and shelter: Meeting the special needs of homeless mentally ill persons—Proceedings of regional meetings*. Rockville, MD: National Institute of Mental Health.

Weissman, H. H. (1978). *Integrating services for troubled families: Dilemmas of program design and implementation*. San Francisco: Jossey-Bass.

chapter 7

The Unique Needs and Concerns of Homeless Women

Mark Rhyns, BS, and
Hoang-Oanh Rodgers, MA

> Constance, 23, is a single mother who has been homeless for 18 months. She lost her job 2 years ago and has been unsuccessful in finding another. Constance has an 11th-grade education. Prior to her 3-week stay at the women's shelter, Constance lived with relatives and friends and in three other shelters in the Maryland and District of Columbia area. Constance has two children, 1 and 3 years of age. Both are presently in foster care, and Constance is hopeful that this is her last shelter and her children will be returned to her soon.

Constance fits the profile of many women who experience the trauma of homelessness. Many are separated from their homes, their belongings, their family support, and, in some cases, their children. This chapter identifies the unique needs and concerns of homeless single women, pregnant women, women with children, abused women, and mentally ill women. It discusses the resources required to meet the unique needs of homeless women and highlights a model program that is successfully addressing these needs.

WHO ARE THE HOMELESS WOMEN?

Women constitute 17 to 20% of homeless poor and disenfranchised people, and the state of the economy is causing more and more heads of households to join the ranks of the unemployed (Burt & Cohen, 1989; Wright, 1989). Because women now head more households, we can conclude that more women will be affected by homelessness. The average education of homeless women is 8th to 11th grade, and over half of these women are single. Forty-seven percent are Black, and 43% are White (Burt & Cohen, 1989).

Homeless single women are often victims of abandonment by their families, usually after repeated incidences of undesirable behavior. They are homeless for periods that range from 3 months to several years. Drug abuse and alcohol abuse are common among these women. Other homeless women are victims of the economy and of physical, sexual, and mental abuse.

> Angela is 20 years old. She was laid off from a secretarial job in Minneapolis. She lost her apartment and had to sell everything. She was sent to a shelter after a nurse found her sleeping in an empty hospital bed. (Orr, 1990)

Homeless single pregnant women often have backgrounds similar to those of homeless women. However, they do have a unique problem because they need prenatal care and regular nourishing meals in order to keep the risk of complications for the infant and themselves at a minimum.

> Brenda was pregnant with twins when she was referred to the Mothers program in the District of Columbia. She was not the typical woman who lived on public assistance. She appeared to have come from an upper middle class background. She had 2 years of college. Brenda got involved with drugs, and her family disowned her. She moved to Washington, DC, and her parents took her children. She was referred to a drug rehabilitation program.

Homeless single women with children also have backgrounds like those of homeless single and single pregnant women. Many are long-term AFDC users, and the majority of their children are 5 years old or younger. Typically, most homeless mothers have inadequate social supports, and some may have been abused as children or battered as adults. Because these women have established families, it is more difficult for them to receive aid from relatives. Adolescent children are usually separated from the family due to age limitations on children in emergency shelters.

> Cynthia had three children when she entered the shelter; however, her mother was providing care for the children. She was pregnant with her fourth child and was a known substance abuser. She had no responsibility for her actions. Cynthia would leave the shelter at eight in the morning and miss all of her case management appointments. She delivered her baby and was back on the streets abusing

> drugs within 2 weeks. . . . Her mother just could not handle another child. . . .

Abused women are yet another subgroup of this homeless population. These are women who have been physically, mentally, or sexually abused. They become homeless when there appears to be no other alternative. The abuser often lives in the same house with them, and the only way they can escape the abusive behavior is to leave the security of their homes.

> Diane was 22 when she successfully left the shelter with her baby. She was not an alcoholic or substance abuser. There was a history of physical and sexual abuse from an uncle in her background. This forced her to leave home in search of some stability in her life. She moved from place to place. Her plans to attend beauty school were ruined when she learned that she was pregnant again. Four months after leaving the shelter, pregnant again. . . .

Twenty percent of homeless women are mentally ill. Professors of psychiatry at the University of Southern California School of Medicine and the University of Maryland School of Medicine concluded that mentally ill people possess certain characteristics that make them vulnerable to homelessness. Those suffering from illnesses such as schizophrenia and manic depression cannot cope with the stresses of life (Orr, 1990).

> Elaine was an individual trying to get off drugs for the fifth or sixth time. She was at St. Elizabeth's Hospital for a while and was borderline schizophrenic. She had good days and bad days. Elaine lived most of her life in public housing. She was in her mid 30s and destitute. Through support and case management, she had remained drug free successfully for 6 months!

Although alcohol and drug abuse is cited most often as the reason for women becoming homeless, it is not the sole factor. Broken family relationships, loss of employment, financial problems, lack of affordable housing, mental illness, physical abuse, sexual abuse, and poor physical health can all be factors that contribute to the state of homelessness that these women experience.

UNIQUE NEEDS AND CONCERNS OF HOMELESS WOMEN

The primary needs of homeless women are shelter and food. However, depending on the woman's situation, the uniqueness of the needs may vary. For example, a single woman with a child will not be admitted to a shelter for single women unless she is willing to split up her family. And a homeless mother with an adolescent male child must also separate from her children because many shelters serving families do not allow male parents and boys over 12 to be sheltered with the mother.

Single homeless women need financial assistance, job training, and support groups as well as food and shelter. These women may or may not be aware of resources that are available to them. A case manager assigned to them will usually apprise them of the particular resources currently available. Women admitted to emergency shelters are concerned about temporary and permanent residence. They are concerned about the next meal. Most are concerned for their safety. The rate of sexual assault on homeless women is 20 times the rate among women in the general population (Wright, 1989).

Homeless pregnant women have some of the same needs and concerns as single homeless women. The basic needs for food and shelter may overshadow the mother's immediate need for prenatal care, and homeless pregnant women are at high risk of developing pregnancy complications because of poor nutrition and limited access to prenatal care. If there is a history of drug abuse, there is also concern about the effects of the drug upon the unborn child: Typical results of extensive drug use during pregnancy include low birth weight, shakes, small head size, and circulatory problems.

Women with children face the possibility of being separated from their family. Homeless mothers realize the importance of keeping the family together and maintaining some degree of stability and normalcy in the lives of their children. Homeless mothers tend to be young, and their rates of mental disorder and substance abuse are relatively low. Previously only about half of these women received aid for dependent children (Wright, 1989), but today the majority of homeless mothers are long-term AFDC users. These women are concerned about job placement and day care for their small children. In many states, kindergarten is mandatory for children 5 years of age. Usually the programs are half a day in length. Many homeless mothers cannot look for housing and employment as well as maintain scheduled appointments because of the need to be at school by dismissal time. Case managers assigned to their cases realize that training sessions, seminars, and other daily activity may be impacted if adequate day care is not provided. Some homeless mothers are even afraid to seek services for fear their children will be taken away from them.

Abused women need medical attention and psychological help. Many are concerned for their life. They need case managers because they are so distraught they have no idea what they need or how to attain it.

Job training is essential for them to maintain their independence. These women are concerned about making it on their own.

The mentally ill homeless women are not able to cope with the stresses of daily life. They need medical attention because drugs help to stabilize their condition. Poor judgment and the state of disarray associated with their illness causes them to lose benefits that they may have been receiving (Orr, 1990). The lack of medical care and the effects of alcohol and other drug abuse further complicate their condition. These women need to be monitored on a consistent basis. It is not clear what their concerns are other than shelter, food, and medical attention.

RESOURCES FOR HOMELESS WOMEN

The subgroups of homeless women clearly have a wide array of needs. The most obvious aid for all is temporary and permanent shelter; but food, financial aid, and medical attention are also high on the list. These women need the structure and organization that case managers and support groups bring to their lives. They all need job training and a linkage with support systems. Women with children must have day care provided for their children and a shelter that allows them to maintain the family unit. Abused and mentally ill homeless women are in need of psychiatric services and counseling. In addition, an equivalent need exists for better coordination of the health care system (including physical and mental health as well as alcohol and drug programs) with the larger social services system (Wright, 1989). Because of the fragmented nature of social services, the most effective means of coordination of services for homeless women are aggressive case management and advocacy to address their unique needs.

There are many who will ask What does it cost to operate shelters, kitchens, missions, health care facilities, and other specific centers (for example, for day care) for homeless women? This is a difficult question to answer. One thing is certain, however: If we do not address the problem now, whatever the cost, it will more than double in the future.

Private institutions take active roles in supporting programs and shelters for homeless people. Many churches donate time, money, and goods to shelters all over America, but this is still not enough to address the many needs of the hundreds of thousands of Americans who become homeless each year. Charitable organizations, foundations, and such organizations as the United Way are all providers of goods and labor to aid homeless people. There are shelters for single homeless women, battered women, single pregnant women, women with children, and drug rehabilitation facilities. Unfortunately, these shelters are constantly filled to capacity.

Several states have received a Robert Wood Johnson Health Care for the Homeless grant to assist with addressing health care needs (Burt & Cohen, 1989). In Cleveland, Ohio, the city sponsors the Downtown Drop-In Center—a unique center that is both a clinic and a center where homeless individuals can spend the day. The center provides day shelter, primary health care, respite care, nursing care, employment counseling, substance abuse counseling, case management, mental health counseling, rest rooms, and referral services. In 1983, 63% of a shelter's operating expenses were paid for by private sources. In addition, 35% of meal services in soup kitchens and shelters are operated by volunteers, and cash donations from individuals in the community represent the most substantial source of income for shelters that are primarily privately operated (Burt & Cohen, 1989).

Some states have created programs to help support homeless people, but other states have done little or nothing to establish such programs. Homelessness is a problem that extends beyond local boundaries. Congress has acknowledged this, and the 1987 Stewart B. McKinney Homeless Assistance Act (Public Law 100-77) involved federal resources that were exclusively directed to aiding the homeless.

In order for homeless women to have a chance of surviving and reentering mainstream society successfully, case management is essential. Case managers serve as advocates to help homeless women get the services they need. Most programs do not have a case management component, however, and homeless women are left to travel from place to place in hopes of getting their needs met.

A MODEL PROGRAM: THE HOUSE OF RUTH, WASHINGTON, DC

The mission of the House of Ruth is to provide shelter and programming for women who are homeless and in the greatest need for services. It is a nonprofit organization supported by private institutions, organizations, and concerned citizens, and it provides services 24 hours a day. Its specific programs for meeting the unique needs of the women who come seeking assistance include:

- **Madison Emergency Shelter**—the main emergency shelter for single women. A woman may receive services on a walk-in basis. A special room is reserved for elderly clients who may need extra care. In addition, a medical center is located on the premises to address any medical needs of the women.

- **Herspace**—a domestic violence center for battered women and their children.
- **Unity**—the transitional program for single women. The majority of these women are employed, but they cannot afford housing.
- **Mothers**—a program for single expectant women in recovery of substance abuse.
- **Kidspace**—a day care program for children of parents who are living in shelters.

Staff for these programs include program coordinators, case managers, life coaches, psychiatrists, medical teams, and other support groups. The administrative team includes the executive director and deputy directors.

Comprehensive and individualized case management services are a significant component for addressing the unique needs of homeless women who may seek help at any one of these programs. Case managers are responsible for determining the needs of the client, identifying support services, helping the client receive needed services, and providing follow-up to ensure that the client is successful in achieving the goals the client has established. The needs of the client are varied: medical assistance, prenatal care, psychiatric care, job training, housing search, support groups, public assistance, child care, and transportation.

The Madison Emergency Shelter houses 138 women. Any single woman can get shelter for the night—as long as there is space available.

Herspace has two programs. One program provides shelter up to 60 days to help stabilize the abused woman and her children. The second program provides transitional shelter in an apartment setting. Four women and their children are placed in individual apartment units that are supervised by program staff who reside in the apartment building. Both programs provide counseling, support, and other services that assist the women and their children to become independent.

Unity is the transitional program specifically set up for single women who have found employment but still can not afford their own apartment. These women have moved from the Madison Emergency Shelter to a more independent setting. The case managers have determined that these women are ready to accept the responsibility of maintaining their own lives. The next step for these women will be to move to their own apartment.

The Mothers program provides services to single expectant mothers who have been referred to the program by a drug treatment center. The women have made a commitment to get off drugs, and they are monitored to see if they are remaining drug free. The women are expected to follow their aftercare plans, which consist of weekly meetings at AA/NA (Alcoholics Anonymous and Narcotics Anonymous) groups, and to report back to their treatment center for scheduled support groups. In addition, the program provides prenatal care, parental training, access to job training programs, GED tutoring, and other services reflective of the women's individual needs.

Kidspace, the day care center for children whose parents live in shelters, provides a stable environment. The teachers provide socialization, skill building, language development, and lots of love. While the children are in the center, the parents are free to look for jobs or participate in job training programs. The age limitation for the program is 2 years to school age.

SUMMARY

Homeless women have many unique needs and concerns. Every Constance, Brenda, Cynthia, Diane, and Elaine has a story to tell and needs, spoken or unspoken, that require considerable thought in order to respond to them successfully. Unfortunately, with the growth of the homeless population and the lack of model programs available to meet the needs of our homeless people, the victory over homelessness in America is currently not in sight. Hoang-Oanh Rodgers, one of this chapter's authors and the program coordinator of the House of Ruth Mothers program, has expressed it this way:

> I think more programs like the House of Ruth would tremendously help our homeless women. I also think that more transitional programs are needed to get homeless women back on their feet. I've always had this dream that instead of supporting a woman for the rest of her life on public assistance, we would give her what she needs after she completes a program, like Mothers, to get her going and gradually decrease the assistance (a weaning process). We have clients who are successfully reentering the mainstream society, but we need more. All we can do is hold on to those success stories as long as possible.

Homeless people are evident in virtually every metropolitan area in the country. They sleep on park benches, huddle in doorways, and regularly frequent public libraries during colder weather. City grates offering warm air ventilation are preferred sleeping locations and sometimes necessary for survival. The breakdown of traditional social structures, relationships, and responsibilities has resulted in many people being placed on the street (Orr, 1990).

Unless we set up more model programs—such as the Downtown Drop-In Center in Cleveland, Ohio, or the House of Ruth programs in Washington, DC—that respond to meet the collective needs of our homeless people, we are fighting a losing battle. We do not know what the future holds in the balance for us, nor how the pendulum of fate will swing. However, the action we set in place for our homeless people today may very well soften the impact of life tomorrow.

REFERENCES

Burt, M.R., & Cohen, B.E. (1989, July). *America's homeless: Numbers, characteristics, and programs that serve them* (Urban Institute Report 89-3). Washington, DC: Urban Institute Press.

Dudley, W. (Ed.). (1988). *Poverty.* St. Paul, MI: Greenhaven Press.

Orr, L. (Ed.). (1990). *The Homeless.* San Diego, CA: Greenhaven Press.

Wright, J.D. (1989). *Address unknown: The homeless in America.* New York: Aldine de Gruyter.

chapter 8

Practical Counseling Techniques: A Training Guide for Counseling Homeless Families

Willie Mae Lewis, PhD

A review of information on homelessness indicates a growing population of homeless people within the United States. Renewed interest in this population has produced more and better information and changed the view of homeless people as only skid row bums. Among homeless people today there is an influx of younger non-White individuals (Crystal & Goldstein, 1984; Wood, Schlossman, Hayashi, & Valdez, 1989), of alcoholic teenagers, and of individuals suffering from mental illnesses. The numbers of homeless women are rapidly increasing, particularly single heads of household and battered women (Merves, 1986), within Latin-American and African-American communities. In addition, homeless people increasingly include runaways, throwaways, and, importantly, families (Hopper & Hamberg, 1984; Mills & Ota, 1989).

This chapter focuses on practical counseling techniques and is designed as a tool for those who work with homeless families. It can be adapted to serve as a basis for curriculum development and training activities to help counselors, educators, social workers, and other helping professionals to address effectively the long- and short-term needs of homeless families. It also contains valuable insights and information for helping professionals who work with or are considering working with homeless families.

The content is based on writings and research (for example, Axelson & Dail, 1988, and McCall, 1990) and on surveys conducted by the author. Four major content areas are addressed: issues and key concerns of homeless families; relationship building, with emphasis on developing trust and connecting emotionally with homeless families; intervention methods for promoting effective change in homeless families; and activation, maintenance, and reinforcement of positive change in homeless families. Curriculum objectives, curriculum content (including suggestions for generating discussion and appropriate references), and exercises for training participants are provided for each area.

ISSUES AND KEY CONCERNS OF HOMELESS FAMILIES

The process of becoming homeless creates a high level of stress for both parents and children. Emotional and financial supports are diminishing. Embarrassment and the sense of loss of identity and self-esteem are increasing. Major stressors include actually being homeless, having to live with strangers, lack of privacy, loss of possessions, and exposure of family secrets and habits. Once a family leaves their residence, they are also often not able to secure benefits because of residence requirements for public assistance. Parents fear they will lose their children to child protective services; and if the children are taken to child protective services for help, their parents fear they will not be able to retrieve them. Creating a safe and definable environment becomes increasingly important for family survival.

Curriculum Objectives

- To understand some of the historical, political, social and economic factors that have contributed to homelessness.
- To understand the diverse needs of homeless families.

Curriculum Content

- Discuss background information on issues of homelessness and identify continuing economic and cultural themes associated with social responses to homelessness. Focus particularly on the need of school systems to respond appropriately to the growing population of homeless children. Schools need to compile data on these students for the purpose of monitoring their academic progress, and this monitoring information should be shared between schools and between school districts in order to keep homeless children from getting lost in the system. (See Johnson & Kreiger, 1989; Lewis & Meyers, 1989.)
- Outline process stages of homelessness and factors contributing to the make-up of this population. (See chapters 1, 2, and 3.)
- Identify types of homeless people and the effectiveness of the local political and related organizations. (See chapters 1, 2, and 3.)
- Outline reasons for the eviction of people within low-income groups, such as welfare changes, cut backs in benefits, replacement of low-cost housing by higher priced housing. Also outline changes in institutional patterns in the treatment of mental illness. (See Knickman & Weitzman, 1989.)
- Outline the relationship between drug and alcohol use. Review why alcohol tends to be the most frequently abused substance and emphasize how addiction affects subsequent decision making. Substance abuse is related to homelessness in that it interrupts the client's ability to take care of necessities such as utilities and rent. (See Ryback & Bassuk, 1986.)
- Discuss family organizational styles and review related family styles that lead to stress. In addition, discuss factors that affect family members' use of their strengths, particularly the restricting of emotions and the lowering of levels of intimacy as a self-protection mechanism. (See Hoffman, 1981.) Explore the relationship of family dynamics to this cycle of homelessness, to low-income groups, and particularly to women and women who are diagnosed as mentally ill.
- Assist learners in determining appropriate and inappropriate responses to these stressors.
- Give specific attention to concepts and resulting effects of mental illness for homeless women. Review issues of diagnosis and misdiagnosis for women and of social styles of resistance to assistance under the label of mental illness. (See Wood et al., 1989.)

Exercises

- Describe the life of a homeless person.
- Write a paragraph on a homeless person you have seen. Include observations, perceptions, and fears. (Note: Participants may need help processing the needs and motivations of homeless people as well as their own stereotypes about homeless people.)
- Brain storm to explore the myths and realities of homelessness. List names of a substance(s) you have used, chart the effects, and identify factors of relapse in the change process.
- Undertake a 1-week observation of homeless families, for example, at a train station or at a community or medical center, and see how they may acquire drugs.

RELATIONSHIP BUILDING

Relating to homeless individuals and families requires developing a sensitivity to their plight, a sensitivity that is not engrossing and sympathetic but rather caring and empathetic. Learning why individuals and families experience homelessness and recognizing that interacting individual and sociological events are major factors in homelessness help develop such sensitivity. Understanding the coping mechanisms for survival leads to understanding the differences between homeless people in shelters and homeless people on the streets.

Becoming an effective helper means learning how interactions are defined by preexisting attitudes as well as learning how to create conditions that help homeless individuals and families feel better about themselves. Effective helpers need to be able to convey their understanding of a homeless individual's or family's self-worth as well as of the individual's or family's dysfunction.

Building trust is essential in building a foundation for a working relationship. Individuals and families should be treated with respect. Determining what made family members proud of themselves prior to their homelessness and demonstrating a valuing of those strengths is important. The family should be responded to in terms of the family's perception of needs. Imagining the situation from the family's point of view will help to clarify the scope of the problem.

In building relationships, counselors should promise no more than they can deliver and provide follow through for. They must be consistent. Counselors should also:

- Describe their goal and function without excuses, and explain to the client the role and functions of other helping persons involved in the process prior to and after the intervention.
- Limit the use of humor because humor is usually therapeutic only when counselors reference themselves or some situation they have encountered.
- Remember they are working with persons whose stress levels may be high enough to provoke anger responses and a loss of temper. Counselors must have the ability not only to delay the gratification of responding immediately but must also be able to respond to an angry or out-of-control response by giving it structure, directiveness, and purpose for the family.

Curriculum Objectives

- To provide experiences for considering the special situations that influence relationships between counselors and homeless individuals and families.
- To introduce skills of connecting through listening and responding verbally and nonverbally.

Curriculum Content

- Outline ingredients for building and maintaining positive relationships as well as methods for reinforcing respect, strengthening empathy, ensuring role clarity, and setting limits of responsibilities. Include verbal and nonverbal expressions of concern and care. Give specific attention to skill development in areas that help the counselor empower the client. This counseling skill will enable clients to identify their own strengths and develop the capacity to engage in self-control during the period of homelessness.
- Review the cultural factors that influence perceptions, interactions, empathy, and individual receptivity to interventions. Define and discuss ethnicity, cultural diversity, cultural discrimination, prejudice, and racism. Outline within context the relationship of these factors to homelessness and the economy. Review group barriers to homelessness when accessing housing and employment (race, gender, number of children).

Exercises

- Identify how you functioned in your family of origin. Discuss communication patterns that were most and least helpful in developing perceptions of belongingness.
- Identify family roles and positions in the family. Review belief systems and cultural identity as indicated within homeless and traditional populations.
- Review and list factors contributing to family homelessness (i.e., marital discord, separation, divorce, and/or physical abuse).

INTERVENTIONS FOR CHANGE

A major aspect of working with homeless families is to stimulate their behavior toward desired change. Although the family's homeless situation may have been shaped by many factors, including job changes, discrimination, and changes in the economy, personal changes by family members may be necessary to generate the desired family changes. The stress generated by their homeless status and the related symptoms, for example, mood disorders, relapses into substance abuse, and children's acting out behaviors, need to be overcome.

Effective interventions with homeless individuals and families are based on observation and assessment of types of behaviors. Such an approach enables counselors to view and assist homeless families in terms of their internal strengths, and it diverges from the typically medical model in which weaknesses are the major areas targeted for interventions. By assessing family functioning, by observing behaviors and expressions among family members and with counselors, this approach addresses not only interactions but also the physical, developmental, and emotional status of individual family members and the family as a unit.

Observation and assessment strategies as well as interviewing techniques are essential elements of this approach.

Curriculum Objectives

- To provide individual and organizational strategies for client change.
- To identify behaviors associated with failure cycles.
- To list practices that demonstrate client advocacy with schools and organizations.

Curriculum Content

This content overview focuses on information and experiences that can create individual desire for change.

- Review information on family functioning, highlighting dysfunction and methods of disconnecting unproductive behavioral cycles.
- Explore how to promote change and how to maximize client strengths (for example, valuing and providing day-to-day survival skills). Specific skills to introduce and reinforce include:
  —structuring an interview to assess motivation for change
  —making client referrals for change
  —setting limits with clients
  —discussing worker ethics and specific policies for the homeless with clients
  —relationship building for team development
  —understanding organizational structure and procedures for developing supportive relationships and for employing organizations in a systematic approach to helping. (See Hutchinson, Searight, & Stretch, 1986.)
- Provide information on mental illness and loss of housing.
- Outline the typical process of events that results in homelessness.
- Discuss and present information on heightened conflict with and supervision of children. Include educational difficulties resulting from frequent absences, school relocation, and disruptive behavior as well as parents' work performances. Discuss loss as an ongoing issue and the related feelings of abandonment by friends and loved ones. Describe possible major mood disturbances, including depression and anxiety-related disorders (for example, claustrophobia). Discuss the physical health issues (including AIDS) as related to emotional changes and self-perceptions. (See Waldinger, 1986.)

Observation and Assessment Strategies

In order to assess a homeless family's motivation for change, and to strengthen the parental role in the family, helpers should first identify the desired change(s) and acknowledge this with the family. Helpers should also:

- Determine what problems the homeless family may have.
- Determine how the family makes decisions and what part the children have in the decision-making process.

- Determine whether certain behaviors ensure family cooperation and how the children attain attention (for example, by arguing while the parents decide on actions to be taken). This determination relates to family organizational style and will be helpful in making treatment decisions as well as in assigning housing.
- Ask questions about and observe who initiates a request for assistance: The family member reacting to homelessness in a responsible manner is usually the most stressed out.
- Give attention to how the family demonstrates affection, particularly under acute stress.
- Determine how the homeless family completes the tasks required for changes perceived as needed. Determine how closely they are working together to resolve their problems.
- Determine if the behavior of family members observed seems appropriate for the situation. Determine:
  —whether the behavior secures attention from others
  —what the function of the behavior is
  —if the behavior distinguishes them from other family members
  —what the effect of the behavior of the helper is
  —whether the behavior brings people closer or sends them away.

Assessing physical-medical status. Homeless families are more likely to be ill than other families. The children are more likely to experience neurological disorders, gastrointestinal disorders, seizures, and asthma. Stressful living in temporary housing creates conditions for many contractible diseases—as well as for emotional disorders (Lewis, 1991; Waldinger, 1986). It is important that the initial assessment of a homeless family's needs include medical needs observations: Determine immunization needs or secure the children's immunization records. Make a list of information for individual medical and school records. Identify previous illnesses as well as recurring skin irritations and colds. Make observations on personal hygiene. Determine if family members drink, where, and how often. Give special attention to any developmental delays as well as medical disorders, and review previous records on such indications as language skills, motor coordination, and school attendance. Also important, of course, is to determine food preferences, eating patterns over time, and nutritional status. This kind of information assists in diagnosing, treating, and planning for recovery.

Assessing emotional status. As already noted, living in temporary housing is stressful and may lead to emotional disorders. The inability of parents, on many occasions, to maintain order or to control their children and life style creates intense feelings of helplessness and consequent periods of depression and family fragmentation. It is important for helpers to observe behavioral patterns in homeless families: Make observations on bonding among family members and types of fears. Determine the extent, if any, to which the children regress, as demonstrated by trying to suck their thumbs or tongues, by holding the thumb or finger of a parent for long periods of time, or by developing bladder or bile control problems. Are the children comfortable when in small groups or in large groups? Does their behavior indicate depression? Are there gaps in memory of time and place? All such information is helpful in diagnosing, treating, and planning the recovery process.

Particular attention should be given when withdrawal occurs, when mood swings are intense, when agitation is present, and when medication is not being taken as prescribed. A major area for assessment is the thinking process and the degree to which homeless family members are able to verbalize coherent thoughts. Helpers who note or observe these and other questionable behaviors should contact a staff member experienced with severe mental disorders.

Some of the more noticeable disorders associated with homelessness are compulsive behaviors such as excessive hand washing and skin rubbing. Associated behaviors are opening sores by mutilating scabs and pulling out eyelashes.

Phobias are a pronounced disorder of many homeless adults and children. Those suffering from sociophobia—the fear of being looked at by people, particularly while eating—generally avoid social situations. Claustrophobia and acrophobia are also common (Lewis, 1991).

The most prevalent disorder experienced by homeless individuals, however, is posttraumatic stress, which prevents these people from developing comfortable interpersonal relationships. The onset of this disorder is associated with loss issues: loss of home, loss of friends, loss of financial security, loss of familiar surroundings. Loss may be ongoing because shelter policies may require separating children, spouses, and extended family members.

When a mental illness brings about the family's homelessness, the stress of being homeless increases the difficulties experienced by the disturbed person. Children who are disturbed are typically noisy and may damage the property of other people. Community conflicts with their parents are heightened because of feelings for family members, behaviors affecting neighbors, self-mutilating behaviors, and fights with teachers and other persons of authority. Phobias concerning schools and other institutions representing power are prevalent with these children.

Most of these difficulties are eliminated with medical and psychological treatment, however. Usually when a family enters family therapy and secures permanent housing, feelings of stability are reclaimed and may be observed.

Interviewing Strategies

Questions are the basic mechanism for interviewing. The timing and type of questions let homeless individuals and families know that the helpers are interested in them and can contribute to a trusting relationship. Because homeless individuals and families generally feel powerless, a slower frequency of questions is required. Frequent questioning typically elicits resistant behavior. Ask one question at a time. Avoid asking another question until an answer is received. This allows the homeless individual to think, to not feel interrogated, and to increase trust.

Typically, open-ended questions are more helpful at the beginning of an interview as the purpose of the interview is discussed. However, with homeless families a nontraditional approach can be helpful, and "Why did you" type questions must be used with care. Before asking questions, share with the homeless individual or family what happens to the information being sought and how the information will help them and their family.

An initial use of closed-end questions, particularly around sensitive topics such as money issues and sexual relations, is not helpful. Homeless individuals tend to feel cornered and will respond in a manner they think the helper wants.

For children, take special care in structuring the interview, and be sure to set some rules for talking with them during the process. Consider age and developmental level. Using open-ended questions is generally more helpful in securing information, particularly if other family members are near by.

The structure of helping organizations and programs may be perceived as conflicting with family functioning and be a source of additional stress for homeless individuals and families. Thus while interviewing the helper should explain to the homeless individual or family the policies and expectations of each contact organization. Rules for participation in any program—for example, for child care or substance abuse—must be made clear and requirements well defined. To enable easier access to services, it is helpful to underline in color key points on any written material given to family members.

Homeless families may request that the helper let them establish residence in the helper's own home. Early in the interview it is important to make agency policies, rules, and regulations clear in order to circumvent this kind of emotional connection. Such a strategy prevents feelings of rejection and protects both the helper and the homeless individual or family.

Often the helper has the responsibility to assist parents in establishing how important it is for the children to follow the rules. Such rules for success usually are stated in writing, as are penalties for not following the rules. The helper should cover each rule, each step for the family's process of recovery. Particularly helpful is to underline in color all written statements of behaviors for positively accomplishing each program phase.

Exercises

- Provide a case scenario with family description and interaction. Include brief background information on the family, presenting issues, information on how the family received homeless status, and information on coping patterns.
- Divide group into dyads. Have one take the role of the counselor and the other of a homeless family. Ask the counselor to outline observations and assessment of major difficulties and the physical and emotional status of individuals and family. Have each counselor practice connecting skills—voice tone, expressions of trust, topic changes—when assisting these families. Review their reactions and methods of responding with suggestions. Discuss various intervention options and counselor perceptions as a connecting force.

APPLICATION AND MAINTENANCE

To activate change behavior and aid homeless families in counterbalancing self-defeating actions, helpers must apply the often-sporadic information derived from assessment. Emphasis should be placed on giving the families a vision of their strengths, on remobilization and stabilization of the families and their individual members. Action strategies should be introduced to both maintain and reinforce life-style changes and community resource connections for family needs and growth.

Curriculum Objectives

- To aid families in identifying ways of circumventing destructive behaviors that break their connecting resources.

- To help families modify perceptions that serve to increase stress.
- To assist in the development of realistic steps for reinforcement and maintenance of stability.
- To help family members monitor strengths and successful interactions.
- To aid family members in the initiation and practice of effective behaviors.

Curriculum Content

Remobilization

The first phase of application and maintenance is remobilization. Remobilizing a homeless family means activating its members' behavior for change. Different attitudes toward themselves and the requirements for change are needed. After determining what the family's needs are, as they are perceived by the family requesting services, the helper applies this information and initiates the remobilization process by:

- Helping the family understand their losses (which may include the temporary loss of one of the family members because of shelter policy).
- Giving hope for positive change by outlining behavior and time expectations with both parents and children.
- Helping the family understand patterns of behavior within their family as well as of similar patterns in their families of origin. This should allow the family to gain awareness of any repeating, defeating cycles of behavior and the need for timed interventions.
- Helping the family identify their strengths during this period of seemingly unsurmountable stress.
- Identifying substance abuse, child abuse, and emotional disorders experienced by the family and assisting the family to bond for change, that is, to make a workable agreement to survive together in a manner each member can live with.
- Developing specific plans with each family member to counter stress and, as needed, planning treatment for depression and any physical disorder.
- Assisting with parenting under the stress of what is generally perceived to be a catastrophe.
- Aiding the family in organizing a plan of survival and enrichment that includes making school contacts and developing the parenting skills needed to enhance life style during this period.

Stabilization

Following the phase of remobilization is the phase of stabilization. Stabilizing a homeless family requires outreach interventions. Helpers should reinforce maintenance of new skills and provide mechanisms to prevent relapses into debilitating behaviors.

This process of outreach requires implementing plans made with the family about using community resources. This means the helper should be familiar with agencies designed to assist homeless people and contact persons at those agencies. To help provide timely outreach assistance for homeless families, the helper should:

- Monitor the family and its contacts with transient shelters.
- Know where funding for home utilities can be secured before those utilities are cut off.
- Identify the location of temporary and long-term housing for homeless families.
- Have knowledge of treatment and training centers for family stress.
- Be aware of special projects that provide skill training to help families retain their homes and manage budgets and time, or that help family members become proficient in using their time when the family is still on the streets and not yet placed in a shelter.
- Synchronize day care information with the planned work schedule of the parent(s).
- Identify public agencies and organizations for permanent address registry. This will enable homeless family members to initiate job searches and apply for financial assistance.

Close attention should be paid to organizing and giving information to homeless individuals or families as it is needed rather than overwhelming them with information. If possible, the helper should define the priority of agency intervention with the family.

During the stabilizing phase, it is most important for the helper to avoid needing to become "a friend of the family." Because of their experiences of loss, homeless family members are noticeably cautious and distrusting. Similarly, for persons with tense life situations, physical touch (usually helpful in strengthening client relationships) tends to become anxiety provoking because of fear of another loss. (See Lewis, 1991.) However, sitting or standing in close proximity with a family typically sends a message of care and relatedness; and paying specific attention to conversations with children often reinforces assistance given as well as maintenance of family change.

Exercises

- Identify client strengths, family functioning, and observed family role-playing.
- Locate and list community agencies helpful to the homeless. Identify those that employ self-help strategies. Specify the most helpful contact person at each and list all necessary follow-up processes.
- Role-play and discuss productive and unproductive ways of sharing information with other helpers and among agencies.

CONCLUSION

This chapter has outlined four major areas that helping professionals need to address in their work with homeless individuals and families. An understanding of the background issues of homelessness as well as of the diversity of needs of homeless individuals and families is essential. The ability to build relationships based on care and empathy produces the trust required for successful interventions. Building on effective observation and assessment strategies ensures interventions for positive change for individuals, families, and organizations. Applying the information gained to mobilize and stabilize homeless families means that positive life style changes and community connections can be successfully maintained and reinforced.

These four areas are basic in all training activities and curriculum for those who work with homeless individuals and families. They are also basic to many of the counseling techniques used by effective helping professionals in assisting homeless people.

REFERENCES

Axelson, L. J., & Dail, F. W. (1988). The changing character of homelessness in the United States. *Family Relations, 34* 473–469.

Crystal, S., & Goldstein, M. (1984). *Correlates of shelter utilization: One-day study.* New York: Human Resources Administration of the City of New York.

Hoffman, L. (1981). *Foundation of family therapy.* New York: Basic Books.

Hopper, K., & Hamberg, J. (1984). *The making of America's homeless: From skid row to new poor.* New York: Community Service Society.

Hutchinson, W. J., Searight, P., & Stretch, J. J. (1986). Multidimensional networking: A response to the needs of homeless families. *Social Work, 31*(6), 427–430.

Johnson, A. K., & Kreiger, L. W. (1989). Toward a better understanding of homeless women. *Social Work, 34*(6), 537–540.

Knickman, J. R., & Weitzman, B. C. (1989). *A study of homeless families in New York City: Risk assessment models and strategies for prevention*. New York: New York University.

Lewis, W. M. (1991). *A study of homeless families in Delaware: Treatment strategies*. Unpublished manuscript.

Lewis, M. R., & Meyers, A. F. (1989). The growth and development status of homeless children entering shelters in Boston. *Public Health Reports, 104*(3), 247–250.

McCall, K. P. (1990). *Educating homeless children and youth: A sample of programs, policies, and procedures*. Cambridge, MA: Center for Law and Education. (ERIC Document Reproduction Service No. ED 320 991)

Merves, E. (1986). *Conversations with homeless women: A sociological analysis*. Unpublished doctoral dissertation, Ohio State University.

Mills, C., & Ota, H. (1989). Homeless women with minor children in the Detroit Metropolitan Area. *Social Work, 34*(5), 485–489.

Ryback, R. F., & Bassuk, E. L. (1986). *Homeless battered women and their sheltered network*. San Francisco: Jossey-Bass.

Waldinger, R. J. (1986). *Fundamentals of psychology*. Washington, DC: American Psychiatric Association.

Wood, D., Schlossman, S., Hayashi, F., & Valdez, R. (1989). *Over the brink: Homeless families in Los Angeles*. Los Angeles, CA: Assembly Office of Research.

chapter 9

Conclusion: Responding to the Challenge

Peggy Jackson-Jobe, MEd

Tonight hundreds of thousands of adults and children will find themselves sleeping on the streets—in parks, abandoned cars and buildings, campgrounds, shelters, welfare motels, and other makeshift arrangements. Many of these Americans who experience homelessness this year will lose more than their homes. Many will lose touch with an environment that provided them a sense of security, a sense of identity, and a sense of belonging. For these Americans, the crisis of homelessness extends far beyond the immediate food and shelter needs. And it is this diversity of need that poses unique challenges for the helping professional.

Educators, counselors, social workers, and other helping professionals are being challenged to respond to the needs of homeless people, but not within the parameters of traditional methods for delivering services. In order to meet this challenge, helping professionals must develop sensitivity to the unique needs and problems facing homeless adults and children by working closely with them, visiting shelters, seeing the conditions in which they live, and sharing their hopes and fears. The helping professional must first understand that the problems of homelessness are as diverse as the people who are homeless.

No longer can we equate homelessness with the little old bag lady, the skid row drunk, or the old man, wrapped in a blanket, sitting over a grate trying to keep warm. The composition of the homeless population has changed dramatically. The homeless population is now more diverse and includes young mothers on welfare who can not afford to pay for rent with their monthly public assistance allotments and whose names have been on the public housing waiting lists for years. There are unemployed men with families, unable to find work or shelter, living in cars and public parks. There are retired men with no family ties and living on fixed incomes who are unable to afford permanent housing and move about constantly. There are young adults, released from foster care and completely without resources, who are unable to find jobs or a place to live. There are old people, schizophrenics, runaway and throw away teenagers, victims of domestic violence, drug addicts; and there are children who move, with their families, from shelter to shelter and live in overcrowded quarters where families are doubled up. These are the faces of our new homeless people who present unique challenges for the helping professional.

IMPLICATIONS FOR HELPING PROFESSIONALS

Homeless adults and children have complex economic, psychosocial, and health care needs that are fragmentally addressed (or not addressed at all) as they travel from shelter to shelter and agency to agency. The stress of homelessness may leave a homeless individual feeling hopeless, frustrated, and unable to explore options or to establish a plan for preventing or resolving crises. It is the role of the helping professional to assist the homeless client in creating a sense of empowerment.

In order to engage effectively in this process of helping homeless clients to feel good about themselves and to make choices that will have a positive impact on their lives, helping professionals must carefully consider the following points: First, before beginning to work with homeless adults and children, helping professionals should explore and change any negative paradigms or beliefs about homeless people and working with them. Myths and misconceptions about the homeless population can be detrimental to the helping professional's diverse roles as counselor, broker, and advocate for the homeless client.

Second, helping professionals should acquire knowledge about the homeless population and the availability of resources and barriers that may prohibit homeless adults and children from accessing needed resources. Helping professionals can not intervene effectively into the lives of homeless clients without knowing something about the conditions in which they live. They need to understand and be sensitive to the unique needs of racial and ethnic minorities. Awareness and sensitivity training can assist the helping professional in understanding the demographics of homelessness, the complexities of service delivery systems, and the public policy issues that impact the lives of homeless people. However, effective training should go beyond awareness. It should also focus on developing and maintaining support networks for both the homeless client and the helping professional. Establishing formal and informal relationships with other helping professionals in the various agencies and shelters can be helpful when brokering for needed services and providing follow-up for the client. In addition, support groups can help to buffer the stresses and frustrations often encountered.

Third, helping professionals should participate in ongoing skill development training. Special emphasis should be placed on developing the interpersonal and interviewing skills necessary to establish a trusting staff/client relationship that encourages communication and collaboration. Helping professionals can not use strategies and interventions that effectively address the needs of homeless adults and children if homeless clients are not engaged as partners in assessing their needs and setting their own goals. Focus on the strengths of the client, and as you establish your rapport, remember this advice given by a homeless youth:

> Don't make promises you can't keep;
> Be there for the long haul; and
> Don't pity us—treat us with respect.

Skill development training should also provide opportunities for helping professionals to share intervention strategies that have effectively addressed the needs of their homeless clients. In addition, internship experiences and visits to shelters are vital hands-on training tools that can heighten awareness, increase knowledge, and provide an arena for skill building and the application of intervention helping strategies.

The chapters in this book present some of the unique challenges and solutions, and embrace the issue of how to help the increasing number of women, children, men, and families that join the ranks of the homeless each year. For example, the helping professional may encounter any one, if not all, of the following scenarios:

- A homeless father, separated from his family because the shelter can not accommodate males, may exhibit anger, distrust, and even reject help.
- A homeless mother with young children may be distressed about being shuffled from agency to agency, and she may be unable to secure services for her family because of complicated rules, procedures, and forms.

- A homeless child who has repeatedly changed schools because of the school districts' inability or unwillingness to provide transportation may be reluctant to make friends in the new school and may exhibit aggressive behavior.
- A young homeless mother, unable to stay in one place longer than 30 days, may feel powerless when trying to articulate to school officials the special educational needs of her school-age child.
- A single woman, living in emergency shelters and welfare motels, may appear distrusting and frightened because of the limited resources available to single homeless women and the reported incidences of abuse.
- A homeless family, unable to find shelter, may find themselves living in an abandoned car or a public park, cut off from resources, and unable to meet their most basic needs.

Responding to the diverse needs of homeless people calls for the emergence of a counseling professional who is both client sensitive and a skilled enabling model of helping. As indicated in the scenarios, homelessness is more than housing: it is a disconnectedness, a separation from support systems. Therefore, the helping professional's intervention strategies should begin with focusing on the immediate needs and concerns of the homeless client: providing transportation, locating a safe place to sleep for the night, completing forms, arranging a meeting with school officials, providing support by going to a scheduled appointment with the client, and identifying the local soup kitchens and facilities for taking a shower.

The role of helping professionals in intervening with homeless adults and children has been addressed extensively in this book. A major theme that has emerged is that in order to provide effective intervention strategies, the helping professional must be sensitive to the needs of the homeless client, coordinate efforts, be aware of and maintain an ongoing relationship with other agencies that provide a service to homeless people, and provide follow-up when possible. In addition, case management is highlighted as perhaps the most effective intervention for providing comprehensive, continuous, and coordinated services for homeless people. The basic functions of the case management system include client identification and outreach, individual assessment, service planning, linkage with requisite services, monitoring of service delivery, and client advocacy. The helping professional should understand that each of these functions lends itself to a team effort where turfism is irrelevant and the needs of the client are the priority.

THE RESPONSE

The changing demographics of our modern American homeless people and the diversity of their needs imply that the response from helping professionals extends beyond the boundary of direct services. The emerging role of the helping professional as counselor, broker, and advocate demands that helping professionals share information with officials who formulate policies and determine funding for services that impact upon the homeless. Additionally, helping professionals must respond to the call for outreach and future research. A careful review and increase in outreach efforts will ensure that the diverse needs of homeless adults and children are being addressed. Likewise, to validate the effectiveness of emerging intervention models of helping, future research and studies are imperative.

Congress took a major step toward addressing the homeless issue with the enactment of the Stewart B. McKinney Homeless Assistance Act of 1987 (Public Law 100-77) and the McKinney Act Amendments of 1990 (Public Law 101-645). The McKinney Act provides grants to state and local governments to address the shelter, counseling, social services, educational, job training, and medical needs of homeless people. However, the appropriated funding levels are inadequate to address the diverse needs of the increasing number of people who have no place to call home. Public policy decision makers at the local, state, and federal levels need to hear from people who work directly with homeless clients. Information needs to be shared about the numbers of homeless people and their diverse needs as well as about service delivery programs that effectively address long- and short-term needs. Without this information, even the limited amount of funding directed toward initiatives to homeless people may be substantially decreased.

Helping professionals can play a significant role in advocating for homeless adults and children by first understanding how the system works and then collaborating with other professionals and organizations that share their interest regarding homeless people. Empowered helping professionals can work toward empowering homeless clients to ultimately advocate for their own needs. When funding for the Education of Homeless Children and Youth Projects was zeroed out of the 1991 presidential budget and plans were being made to provide nationwide competitive grants to state agencies for McKinney funds, educators, parent groups, and homeless parents and students worked together to heighten the awareness of legislators about the benefits of the project to homeless children. The National Association of State Coordinators for the Education of Homeless Children and Youth produced a position document highlighting case studies of how state projects have helped homeless children across the country, teachers and other school personnel wrote letters to legislators expressing the special needs of homeless children, and homeless parents and students gave personal testimonies before Congress. Congress listened—and the Education for Homeless Children and Youth Project was reinstated with increased funding to ensure that our homeless students have access and success in schools.

Very often, homeless families and individuals who reside in parks and campgrounds, on the streets, and in abandoned buildings and cars are not aware of the procedures for accessing the support services that may be available to them. Helping professionals can ensure awareness of, access to, and delivery of needed services to homeless adults and children by establishing or following through on the outreach efforts of their agency, department, or organization. Outreach efforts may vary depending on funding and the needs of the homeless population in a community. Communities in Texas, New York, Washington, DC, California, and Maryland have effectively implemented the following outreach activities:

- Distribution of fliers, public broadcasting announcements, and an 800 hot-line telephone number that helps to disseminate information and answers questions about homeless children's rights to attend school and the procedures for registration (Texas)
- Mobile health teams that go where homeless families reside to address health care needs (New York)
- Routine scheduled visits by social workers to shelters and welfare motels to assist families with accessing needed resources and to help children with school-related concerns and needs (Washington, DC)
- Mobile learning vans that provide tutorial and homework assistance to children residing on campgrounds (California)
- Weekly visits to a day care facility by a pediatrician and nurse to provide examinations and address health care needs of preschool children (Maryland).

As helping professionals search for the most effective way to address the unique needs of homeless clients, it is quite evident that the traditional methods of service delivery are not appropriate. However, research is still needed to support strategies and interventions that successfully empower homeless clients by changing behaviors, attitudes, and values. Follow-up research is also needed on existing studies to help answer such questions as What works? and Where do we go from here? It is important that evaluation data and findings from research studies are shared with helping professionals and policy decision makers to support the need for continued funding of research activities and innovative initiatives that are effective.

The challenge for helping professionals has been clearly defined. The effectiveness of the response, however, will not be measured by the number of homeless people being serviced. Instead, the effectiveness of the response will be observed in the emergence of helping professionals who address the needs and challenges for meeting the needs of homeless people with unique solutions and sensitivity.

REFERENCES

Bassuk, E. L. (1990). *Community care for homeless families: A program design manual.* Washington, DC: Better Homes Foundation.

Herr, S. (1991). Children without homes: Rights to education and to family stability. *University of Miami Law Review, 45* (2–3).

Hope, H., & Young, J. (1986). *The faces of homelessness.* Lexington, MA: Lexington Books/D.C. Heath.

National Association of State Coordinators for the Education of Homeless Children and Youth. (1991). *Homeless, not hopeless: Ensuring educational opportunity for America's homeless children and youth.* Phoenix, AZ: Author.

Notkin, S., Rosenthal, B., & Hopper, K. (1990, Summer). *Families on the move.* New York: Edna McConnell Clark Foundation.

Russell, B. G. (1991). *Silent sisters, a study of homeless women.* Baltimore, MD: Hemisphere.

Stark, L. (1987). *Homelessness critical issues for policy and practice: Blame the system, not its victims.* Boston: Boston Foundation.

chapter 10

Selected Resources

Compiled by the Research Team of the National Association of State Coordinators for the Education of Homeless Children and Youth

Acker, P. J., Fierman, A. H., & Dryer, B. P. (1987). An assessment of parameters of health-care and nutrition in homeless children. *American Journal of Diseases of Children, 141*, 388.

Allington, R., & Brockov, K. (1988). Development of shared knowledge: A new role for classroom and specialist teachers. *The Reading Teacher.*

Alperstein, G., Rappaport, C., & Flanigan, J. M. (1988). Health problems of homeless children in New York City. *American Journal of Public Health, 78*, 1232–1233.

Anderson, D. (1987, November–December). When the bough breaks. *The Family Therapy Networker*, pp. 18–29.

Andrade, S. J. (1988). *Living in the gray zone: Health care needs of homeless persons.* San Antonio, TX: Benedictine Health Resource Center.

Auletta, K. (1982). *The underclass.* New York: Random House.

Axelson, L., Dail, J., & Paula, W. (1988). The changing character of homelessness in the United States. *Family Relations, 34*, 463–468.

Bassuk, E. L. (1986, June). Homeless families: Single mothers and their children in Boston shelters. *New Directions for Mental Health Services, 30*, 45–53.

Bassuk, E. L. (1987). The feminization of homelessness: Families in Boston shelters. *American Journal of Social Psychiatry, 7*, 19–23.

Bassuk, E. L., & Rosenberg, L. (1988). Why does family homelessness occur? A case control study. *American Journal of Public Health, 78*, 783–788.

Bassuk, E. L., & Rubin, L. (1987). Homeless children: A neglected population. *Journal of the American Orthopsychiatric Association, 57*, 279–286.

Bassuk, E. L., Rubin, L., & Lauriat, A. S. (1986). Characteristics of sheltered homeless families. *American Journal of Public Health, 76*(9), 1097–1101.

Bassuk, E. L., Rubin, L., & Lauriat, A. S. (1986). Is homelessness a mental health problem? *American Journal of Public Health, 76.*

Baxter, E., & Hopper, K. (1982). The new mendicancy: Homeless in New York City. *American Journal of Orthopsychiatry, 52*, 393–408.

Baxter, E., & Hopper, J. (1987). *Private lives/public spaces: Homeless adults on the streets of New York.* New York: Community Services Society.

Bayliss, S. (1987, October 30). One way ticket to Paddington. *The Times Education Supplement.*

Beach, M. E. (1989). *Invisible people: A methodological dilemma.* Unpublished manuscript, University of Vermont.

Beach, M. E. (1989). *You can't get a library card, if you're homeless.* Montpelier: Vermont State Department of Education.

Bingham, R., Green, R., & White, S. (1987). *The homeless in contemporary society.* Newbury Park, CA: Sage.

Birch, E. L. (Ed.). (1985). *The unsheltered woman: Women and housing in the 80s.* New Brunswick, NJ: Center for Urban Policy Research.

The Boston Foundation. (1987). *Homelessness: Critical issues for policy and practice.* Boston: Author.

Bowen, J. M., Purrington, G. S., & O'Brien, K. (1989, March). *Educating homeless children and youth: A policy analysis.* New York State School Boards Association. (ERIC Document Reproduction Service No. ED 307 033.)

Bush, P. (1987). Vermont's invisible people. *Southern Vermont.* (Copies available from N. Beach, Coordinator, Vermont Department of Education.)

Coles, R. (1989, July). Lost youth. *Vogue.*

Campus self-assessment guide for the education of homeless students. (1990). Austin, TX: Texas Education Agency.

Caton, C. L. M. (1989). *Without dreams: The homeless of America.* New York: Columbia University.

Center for Law and Education. (1987). The educational rights of homeless children. *Newsnotes, 38.*

Center for Law and Education. (1987). Homelessness: A barrier to education for thousands of children. *Newsnotes, 38.*

Chandler, B., & Roff, L. L. (1990, October). *Services for homeless children and their families.* Tuscaloosa: University of Alabama.

Chandler, L. A. (1982). *Children under stress.* Springfield, IL: Thomas.

Chauvin, V., Duncan, J., & Marcontel, M. (1989). Homeless students of the 1990s: A new school population. *School Nurse, 6*(3), 10–13.

Chavkin, W., Seabron, C., & Guigli, P. E. (1987). The reproductive experience of women living in hotels for the homeless in New York City. *New York State Journal of Medicine, 87*, 10–13.

Children in shelters. (1986). *Children Today, 15*, 6–25.

Coles, R. (1967). *Children of crisis, Vol. II: Migrants, sharecroppers, mountaineers.* Boston: Little, Brown.

Coles, R. (1970). *Uprooted children.* Pittsburgh, PA: University of Pittsburgh Press.

Coles, R., & Piers, M. (1969). *Wages of neglect.* Chicago: Quadrangle.

Columbia University Community Services. (1988). *Working with homeless people: A guide for staff and volunteers.* New York: Columbia University.

Cooper, M. A. (1988, August). *The new homeless—children and families.* Washington, DC: Prepare.

Coopersmith, S. (1967). *The antecedents of self-esteem.* Palo Alto, CA: Consulting Psychologist's Press.

Cowan, C., Breakey, W., & Fisher, P. (1988). *The methodology of counting the homeless*. Washington, DC: National Academy Press.

deLeone, R. (1979). *Small futures*. New York: Harcourt Brace Jovanovich.

Dement, E. (1985). *Working paper, out of sight, out of mind: An update on migrant farmworker issues in today's agricultural market*. Washington, DC: National Government Association.

Diaz, J., Trotter, R., & Rivera, V. (1990). *The effects of migration of children: An ethnographic study*. State College, PA: Centro de Estudios Sobre la Migracion.

Dobbin, M. (1987, August 3). The children of the homeless. *U.S. News and World Report*, pp. 20–21.

Dropout prevention for homeless and foster care youth: Toward a unified strategy. (1989). New York: Project Gain.

Dunn, J. L. (1985). *Colorado migrant education program, 1973–1974. Summary and evaluation report*. Denver: Colorado State Department of Education, Compensatory Education Unit.

Eddowes, E. A., & Harnitz, J. R. (1989). Educating children of the homeless. *Childhood Education, 65*, 198–200.

Edelman, M. W. (1981). Who is for children? *American Psychologist, 36*, 109–116.

Edelman, M. W. (1987). *Families in peril: An agenda for social change*. Cambridge, MA: Harvard University Press.

Edelman, M. W., & Mihaly, L. (1989). Homeless families and the housing crisis in the United States. *Children and Youth Services Review, 11*, 91–108.

Edmonds, R. (1979). Effective schools for the urban poor. *Educational Leadership, 37*, 15–24.

Educating homeless children and youth: How are we measuring up? (1990). Baltimore: Maryland State Department of Education.

Education for homeless children and youth program. (1990). Washington, DC: U.S. Department of Education.

Ely, L. (1987). *Broken lives: Denial of education to homeless children*. Washington, DC: National Coalition for the Homeless.

Erikson, K. T. (1976). *Everything in its path: Destruction of community in the Buffalo Creek flood*. New York: Simon and Schuster.

Escalona, S. K. (1982). Babies at double hazard: Early development of infants at biologic and social risk. *Pediatrics, 70*, 670–676.

Fadiman, A. (1987, December 30). A week in the life of a homeless family. *Life*, p. 10.

First, R. J., & Arewa, B. D. (1988). Homelessness: Understanding the dimensions of the problem for minorities. *Social Work, 33*, 120–124.

First, P. F., & Cooper, G. R. (1990). The McKinney Homeless Assistance Act: Evaluating the response of the states. *West's Education Law Reporter, 60*, 1046–1060.

Freudenberger, H. J., & Torkelsen, S. E. (1984). Beyond the interpersonal: A systems model of therapeutic care for homeless children and youth. *Psychotherapy—Theory Research and Practice, 21*, 132–140.

Friedman, L., & Christiansen, G. (1990). *Shut out: Denial of education to homeless children*. Washington, DC: National Law Center on Homelessness and Poverty. (ERIC Document Reproduction Service No. ED 320 987)

Fustero, S. (1984). Home on the street. *Psychology Today, 18*, 56–63.

Futrell, M. H. (1988, April). A cruel Catch 22. *NEA Today*, pp. 6, 9.

Gewirtzman, R., & Fodor, I. (1987). The homeless child at school: From welfare hotel to classroom. *Child Welfare, 66*, 237–245.

Goffin, S. G. (1988). Putting our advocacy efforts into a new context. *Young Children, 43*, 52–56.

Goldberg, K. (1988, June 1). New York board sets rules for the homeless. *Education Week*, p. 10.

Gonzalez, M. A. (1991, September). School-community partnerships and the homeless. *Educational Leadership*.

Gonzalez, M. L. (1990). School + home = A program for educating homeless students. *Phi Delta Kappan, 71*(10), 785–787.

Gorder, C. (1988). *Homeless! Without an address in America*. Tempe, AZ: Blue Bird Publishing.

Hard times [excerpt from Homeless in America]. (1988, March 21). *Newsweek*, pp. 46–55.

Harrington, M. (1962). *The other America*. New York: Macmillan.

Harrington, M. (1984). *The new American poverty*. New York: Penguin Press.

Harrington-Lueker, D. (1989, July). What kind of school board member would help homeless children? *American School Board Journal*, pp. 12–19.

Hart, R. (1979). *Children's experience of place*. New York: Irvington.

Hartman, C. (1983). *America's housing crisis*. Boston: Routledge and Kegan Paul.

Haskins, R., & Gallagher, J. J. (1980). *Care and education of young children in America*. Norwood, NJ: Ablex.

Heath, S. B., & McLaughlin, M. W. (1987). A child resource policy: Moving beyond dependence on school and family. *Phi Delta Kappan, 68*, 576–580.

Herbert, M. (1985). *Children of the welfare hotel*. New York: Citizens' Committee for Children.

Hersch, P. (1988, January 22). Coming of age on city streets. *Psychology Today*, pp. 29–37.

Hiratsuka, J. (1989, March 3). Homeless kids face barriers to schooling. *National Association of Social Workers News*.

Hirsch, K. (1989). *Songs from the alley*. New York: Doubleday.

Hombs, M. E., & Snyder, M. *Homeless in America: A forced march to nowhere*. Washington, DC: Community for Creative Non-Violence.

Homeless battered women and their shelter network: The mental health needs of homeless persons. (1986). San Francisco: Jossey-Bass.

Homeless children. (1987, May–June). *Children Today*.

Homeless children and youth: About 68,000 homeless and 186,000 in shared housing at any given time. (1989). Washington, DC: U.S. General Accounting Office.

Authorization vs. appropriation: Legislative update. (1991). *Homeless Education Beam* [Special edition], pp. 5–9. (Available from Office for the Education of Homeless Children and Youth, Arizona Department of Education.)

Homeless families: How they got that way. (1987, November–December). *Society*, p. 25.

Homelessness: Access of McKinney Act programs improved but better oversight needed. (1990). Washington, DC: U.S. General Accounting Office.

Homelessness in America's cities: Ten case studies. (1984). Washington, DC: U.S. Conference of Mayors.

Homelessness Information Exchange. (1987). *Coalition building; Comprehensive city planning; Family and child homelessness; General information; How to get involved in your community; Transitional housing* (information packets). Washington, DC: Author.

Hope, M., & Young, J. (1986). *The faces of homelessness.* Lexington, MA: Lexington Books/D.C. Heath.

Hopper, K. (1984). Whose lives are these, anyway? *Urban and Social Change Review, 17,* 12–13.

Hopper, K., & Hamberg, J. (1984). *The making of America's homeless: From skid row to new poor, 1945–1984.* New York: Community Service Society.

Housing and homelessness: A teaching guide. Washington, DC: Housing NOW.

Housing Assistance Council. (1987). *The homeless crisis from a rural perspective.* Washington, DC: Author.

Hutchison, W. J., Searight, P., & Stretch, J. J. (1986). Multidimensional networking: A response to the needs of homeless families. *Social Work, 31,* 427–430.

Institute of Medicine Staff. (1989). *Homelessness, health, and human needs.* Washington, DC: National Academy Press.

Interagency Council on the Homeless. (1990). *Executive summary of the 1990 annual report.* Washington, DC: Author.

Jackson, S. (1988). *Materials on the education of homeless children.* Cambridge, MA: Center for Law and Education.

Jackson, S. (1988). Report from Washington: Homeless children in America: They need to go to school. *PTA Today, 13,* 27–28.

Jackson, S. (1990). *State plans for the education of homeless children and youth: A selected survey of 35 states.* Cambridge, MA: Center for Law and Education.

James, W. H., Mann, R., & Smith, A. J. (1991). Educating homeless children: Interprofessional case management. *Childhood Education,* pp. 305–308.

Jennings, J. (1989, February 22). Tally of homelessness should be viewed 'with caution,' department concedes. *Education Week.*

Jennings, L. (1988, September 28). Panel says children fastest-growing portion of homeless. *Education Week.*

Johnson, J. F. (1991). McKinney amendments of 1990: Reauthorization highlights. *Homeless Education Beam* [Special edition], pp. 1–4. (Available from Office for the Education of Homeless Children and Youth, Arizona Department of Education.)

Johnson, J. F., Davidson, D., Jackson-Jobe, P., & Linehan, M. (1990). *Position document on the reauthorization of Subtitle VII-B of the Stewart B. McKinney Homeless Assistance Act.* Baltimore, MD: National Association of State Coordinators for the Education of Homeless Children and Youth, Maryland Department of Education.

Johnson, J. F., & Wand, B. (1991). *Homeless, not hopeless: Ensuring educational opportunity for America's homeless children and youth.* Baltimore, MD: National Association of State Coordinators for the Education of Homeless Children and Youth, Maryland Department of Education.

Karlen, N. (1986, January 6). Homeless kids: Forgotten faces. *Newsweek*, p. 20.

Kelley, K. J. (1989). *When are we going to have a regular place to live?* (Vol. 12). Vanguard Press.

Kenkel, M. B. (1986). Stress-coping-support in rural communities: A model for primary prevention. *American Journal of Community Psychology, 14*, 457–458.

King, P. (1987, January 12). A family down and out: Parents and children are the fastest growing segment of the homeless: The consequences of a transient life can bc tragic. *Newsweek*, p. 44.

King-Stoops, J. (1980). *Migrant education: Teaching the wandering ones*. Bloomington, IN: Phi Delta Kappa Educational Foundation.

Knapp, E. S. (1990). *Investing in families*. Lexington, KY: Council of State Governments.

Knauss, J., & Nelson, K. (1986). *Homeless in Chicago: The special case of pregnant teenagers and young parents*. Carbondale: Illinois Caucus on Teenage Pregnancy.

Kozol, J. (1988, January 25). A reporter at large: The homeless and their children (1). *New Yorker*, pp. 65 ff.

Kozol, J. (1988, February 1). A reporter at large: The homeless and their children (2). *New Yorker*, pp. 36 ff.

Kozol, J. (1988). *Rachel and her children*. New York: Crown.

Kozol, J. (1991). *Savage inequalities: Children in America's School*. New York: Random House.

Leslie, C. (1989, January 23). Can a shelter be a school? *Newsweek*, p. 51.

Maggio, T. M. (1989, February 18). Homeless live in our hometown. *Brattleboro Reformer*, p. 7.

Maggio, T. M. (1989, February 20). There's help for the homeless. *Brattleboro Reformer*, p. 8.

Marin, P. (1988, January/February). How we help and harm the homeless. *Utne Reader*.

Maza, P. L., & Hall, J. A. (1988). *Homeless children and their families: A preliminary study*. Washington, DC: Child Welfare League of America.

McCall, K. P. (1990). *Educating homeless children and youth: A sample of programs, policies, and procedures*. Center for Law and Education. (ERIC Document Reproduction Service No. ED 320 991)

McCallum, D. M., Esser-Stuart, J. E., & Lawrence, K. E. Jr. (1991). *Investigation of school-aged children and their families in doubled-up living situations*. Tuscaloosa: University of Alabama, Institute for Social Science Research.

McChesney, K. Y. (1986). Families: The new homeless. *Family Professional, 1*, 13–14.

McChesney, K. Y. (1986). New findings on homeless families. *Family Professional, 1*.

McCubbin, H. I., Cauble, A. E., & Patterson, J. M. (1982). *Family stress, coping, and social support*. Springfield, IL: Thomas.

Meeting the educational needs of homeless children. (1990, March). *Homewords*, pp. 1–3.

Mid-America in crisis: Homelessness in Des Moines. (1986). New York: National Coalition for the Homeless.

Migrant education: A consolidated view. (1987). Denver, CO: Education Commission of the States, Interstate Migrant Education Council.

Mom, our home is any place. (1988). St. Louis, MO: The Kids in Between, Inc.

Moreno, S. (1984, October 25). Plan offers school to hotel kids. *New York Newsday.*

Moroz, K. J., & Segal, E. A. (1990, January). Homeless children: Intervention strategies for school social workers. *Social Work in Education Journal,* pp. 134–143.

Mowbray, C. T. (1985). Homeless in America: Myths and realities. *American Journal of Orthopsychiatry, 55.*

National Institute of Mental Health. *Helping homeless families.* Rockville, MD: Homeless Resource Center.

National Network of Runaway and Youth Services, Inc. *To whom do they belong? A profile of America's runaway and homeless youth and the programs that help them.* Washington, DC: Author. (ERIC Document Reproduction Service No. ED 261 140)

Nixon, D. (1991, January). On the move to nowhere. *The Rotarian,* pp. 24–29.

No place like home: A report on the tragedy of homeless children and their families in Massachusetts. (1986). Boston: Committee for Children and Youth.

No room at the inn: A study of homeless families in Colorado (1987). Denver, CO: Colorado Children's Campaign.

Perchance to sleep: Homeless children without shelter in New York City. (1984). New York: National Coalition for the Homeless.

A place to call home: The crisis in housing for the poor. (1989). Washington, DC: Center on Budget and Policy Priorities and Low Income Housing Information Service.

Proch, K., & Taber, M. A. (1987). Helping the homeless. *Public Welfare, 45,* 5–9.

Rader, V. (1986). *Signal through the flames: Mitch Snyder and America's homeless.* Kansas City: Sheed and Ward.

Rafferty, Y., & Rollins, N. (1989). *Learning in limbo: The educational deprivation of homeless children.* New York: Advocates for Children of New York. (ERIC Document Reproduction Service No. ED 312 363)

Raymond, C. (1990, September 5). Scholarship on homeless gets increased attention from many sociologists and psychologists (1990). *Chronicle of Higher Education.*

Redlener, I. E. (1989, October 4). *Unacceptable losses: The consequences of failing America's homeless children.* Testimony before the U.S. Senate's Committee on Labor and Human Resources, Subcommittee on Children, Family, Drugs, and Alcoholism.

A report to the secretary on the homeless and emergency shelters. (1984). Washington, DC: U.S. Department of Housing and Urban Development.

The right to housing: A blueprint for housing the nation. (1989). Washington, DC: Institute for Policy Studies, Working Group on Housing.

Rios, B. R. (1987). *Selected trends and issues in rural education and small schools.* (ERIC Document Reproduction Service No. ED 289 669)

Rivlin, L. G. (1990). Home and homelessness in the lives of children. *Child and Youth Services, 14*(1) 5–17.

Rodgers, H. R. Jr., (1986). *Poor women, poor families.* Armonk, NY: M. G. Sharpe.

Ross, H. L., & Sawhill, I. V. (1975). *Time of transition: The growth of families headed by women.* Washington, DC: Urban Institute.

Rossi, P. H. (1989). *Down and out in America, the origins of homelessness.* Chicago, IL: University of Chicago Press.

Rousseau, A. M. (1982). *Shopping bag ladies: Homeless women speak about their lives.* New York: Pilgrim Press.

Rudes, B. A., & Willette, J. L. (1990). *Handbook of effective migrant education practices. Vol. 1: Findings.* Arlington, VA: U.S. Department of Education, Office of Planning, Budget, and Evaluation.

Sageor, R. (1988). Discouraged learners teetering on the edge of failure. *Learning, 17*, 28–34.

Schorr, L. B. (1988). *Within our reach.* New York: Doubleday.

Schorr, L. B. (1989). Early interventions to reduce intergenerational disadvantage: The new policy context. *Teachers College Record, 90*, 363–374.

Seabrook, J. (1988, January 8). Making it home. *New Statesman*, p. 115.

Sheldin, A., Klopf, G. J., & Zaret, E. S. (1988). *The school as locus of advocacy for children.* New York: Elementary School Center.

Sidel, R. (1986). *Women and children last: The plight of poor women in affluent America.* New York: Viking Penguin.

Simpson, J., Kilduff, M., & Blewett, C. D. (1984). *Struggling to survive in a welfare hotel.* New York: Community Service Society of New York.

Stengel, R. (1987, November 24). Down and out and dispossessed; many of the new homeless include families and the young. *Time*, p. 27.

Stewart B. McKinney Homeless Assistance Act of 1987. Public Law 100-77. Subtitle VII-B. 42 U.S.C. § 11431–11432.

Stewart B. McKinney Homeless Assistance Amendments of 1990, Public Law 106-645. *Congressional Record*, 136 (148, Part 2).

Stronge, J. H., & Tenhuse, C. (1990). *Educating homeless children: Issues and answers.* Bloomington, IN: Phi Delta Kappa Educational Foundation.

Students in California migrant education programs. (1989). Sacramento: California State Department of Education, Migrant Education Office.

Swerdlow, A., Bridenthal, R., Kelly, J., & Vine P. (1981). *Household and kin.* New York: Feminist Press.

Tower, C. C., & White, D. J. *Homeless students.* Washington, DC: National Education Association.

Uline, C. L. (1991, May 17). *Legislative update.* Baltimore, MD: National Association of State Coordinators for the Education of Homeless Children and Youth, Maryland Department of Education.

U.S. Department of Education (1988). *Nonregulatory guidance on the subtitle VII-B of the McKinney Homeless Assistance Act.* Washington, DC: Author.

U.S. Department of Education. (1987). *What works—schools that work: Educating disadvantaged children.* Pueblo, CO: Schools That Work.

U.S. Department of Education. (1989). *Report to Congress: Education of homeless children and youth—State grants.* Washington, DC: Author.

Vermund, S. H., Belmar, R., & Drucker, E. (1987). Homelessness in New York City: The youngest victims. *New York State Journal of Medicine, 87*, 3–5.

A vision for America's future: An agenda for the 1990s. (1989). Washington, DC: Children's Defense Fund.

Walmer, T. (1989, December 12). Forgotten homeless: Half a million in rural U.S.A. are invisible. *USA Today.*

Ward, M. C. (1986). *Poor women, powerful men.* Boulder, CO: Westview Press.

Waxman, L. D., & Reyes, L. M. (1987). *The continuing growth of hunger, homelessness, and poverty in America's cities: 1987.* Washington, DC: U.S. Conference of Mayors.

Waxman, L. D., & Reyes, L. M. (1988). *A status report on hunger and homelessness in America's cities: 1988.* Washington, DC: U.S. Conference of Mayors. (ERIC Document Reproduction Services No. ED 315 465)

Weiss, S. (1988). No place called home. *NEA Today, 7,* 10–11.

Whitman, D. (1988, February). Hope for the homeless. *U.S. News and World Report,* 25–30.

Whitman, D. (1988, January 11). America's hidden poor. *U.S. News and World Report,* pp. 18–24.

Whitman, B. Y., Accardo, P., Boyert, M., & Kendagor, R. (1990). Homelessness and cognitive performance in children: A possible link. *Social Work, 35*(6), 516–519.

Wiegard, R. B. (1985). *Counting the homeless.* Ithaca, NY: American Demographics.

Wright, J. D. (1989). *Address unknown: The homeless in America.* New York: Aldine de Gruyter.

Wright, J. D., & Weber, E. (1987). *Homelessness and health.* Washington, DC: McGraw-Hill.

Wright, J. D., Weber-Burdin, E., Knight, J. W., & Lam, J. A. (1987). *The national health care for the homelessness program: The first year.* Amherst: University of Massachusetts, Social and Demographic Research Institute.

Zeldin, S., & Bogart, J. (1990). *Education and community support for homeless children and youth: Profiles of 15 innovative and promising approaches.* Washington, DC: Policy Studies Associates. (ERIC Document Reproduction Service No. ED 322 249)

Zigler, E., & Finn, M. (1981). From problem to solution: Changing public policy as it affects children and families. *Young Children, 36,* 55–59.

Videos and Film

Down and out in America [Video]. New York: Joseph Feary Productions, 620 West End Avenue, 10021.

Hope for the future: Educating homeless children and youth [Video]. Los Angeles, CA: California Homeless Coalition and Pacific Telesis Foundation, 1010 South Flower Street, No. 500, 90015.

Lane, C. (Producer). (1989). *Sidewalk stories* [Film]. (Silent, black and white.)

The many faces of homelessness [Video]. Washington, DC: Homebuilders Association.

No place called home [Video]. Nashville, TN: Edufilm, 810 12th Avenue S., 37203.

No room to learn [Video]. Pennsylvania State Department of Education. (Homeless students in New York City and an extended school day program to serve them.)

A place to call home [Video]. Elgin, IL: Global Food Crisis Fund, Brethren Press, 1451 Dundee Avenue, 60120.

Poor kids [Video]. Pennsylvania State Department of Education. (Two- part series on homelessness in Bucks County, including clip on school children.)

Promises to keep [Video]. Washington, DC: Durin Films, 1748 Kalorama Road, N.W., 20008.

Refugee families in our own country [Video]. Reno: University of Nevada, College of Education, RBPC, Room 201, 89557. (An interview with a homeless mother of three.)

Shelter boy [Video] (from *The Reporters*). New York: Fox Television, 205 East 67th Street, 10021.

Where do we go from here? [Video]. Pennsylvania State Department of Education. (Homelessness in the Lehigh Valley.)

Youth at risk [Video]. Pennsylvania State Department of Education. (Focuses on all students at risk and includes a clip on kids in shelters.)

Newsletters

Homeless Education BEAM (newsletter)
National Association of State Coordinators for the
Education of Homeless Children and Youth
Arizona State Department of Education
1535 West Jefferson Street
Phoenix, AZ 85007
(602-255-4361)

Homewords (quarterly newsletter)
Homelessness Information Exchange
1830 Connecticut Avenue, N.W.
Washington, DC 20009
(202-462-7551)

Safety Network (monthly newsletter)
National Coalition for the Homeless
1621 Connecticut Avenue, N.W., Fourth Floor
Washington, DC 20009
(202-265-2371)